THE TAO OF INNOVATION

NINE QUESTIONS EVERY INNOVATOR MUST ANSWER

TENG-KEE TAN • HSIEN SEOW • SUE TAN TOYOFUKU

Imperial College Press

ICP

Published by

Imperial College Press
57 Shelton Street
Covent Garden
London WC2H 9HE

Distributed by

World Scientific Publishing Co. Pte. Ltd.
5 Toh Tuck Link, Singapore 596224
USA office: 27 Warren Street, Suite 401-402, Hackensack, NJ 07601
UK office: 57 Shelton Street, Covent Garden, London WC2H 9HE

Cover and text design: Tania Craan

Illustrations: Michael Arismandez and Tania Craan (pp. xii, xiii, xlvii, 1, 6, 21, 57, 62, 69, 123, 134-135, 140, 141, 150, 165, 183, 221, and 222-223)

Photo credits: Mark McDonald (p iv), S. Wilson (p v), Hsien Seow (p v), Mike Sinclair (pp xv, 203 and 210), James Ewing (pp 18, 204 and 207), pcruciatti (p 22), DDCoral (p 44), Cindy Shebley (p 65), Thor Jorgen Udvang (p 72), Action Sports Photography (p 88), rickyd (p 93), Adriano Castelli (p 94), Sean Wandzilak (p 126), TungCheung (p 144), Oliver Hoffmann (p 146), Joyfuldesigns (p 213), Zvonimir Atletic (p 214), 1000 Words (p 215), and Eric Toyofuku (p 226). All other images are from Shutterstock.

Library of Congress Cataloging-in-Publication Data
Tan, Teng-Kee.
   The Tao of innovation : nine questions every innovator must answer / Teng-Kee Tan,
Hsien Seow, Sue Tan Toyofuku.
      pages cm
   ISBN 978-1-78326-620-3
   1. Strategic planning. 2. Organizational change. 3. Technological innovations. 4. New products. 5. Entrepreneurship. I. Title.
   HD30.28.T3584 2015
   658.4'063--dc23

                                                                    2014033117

British Library Cataloguing-in-Publication Data
A catalogue record for this book is available from the British Library.

Printed in Singapore

This book is dedicated to my dear wife who allowed me to focus my life on intellectual pursuits and my children who are my cheer leaders. It is also dedicated to all my students and those who want to change the world through purposeful innovation.　　　　　　　　　　　　　　—Teng-Kee Tan

To my family, whose constant support gave me wings, and to my wife, whose love has let me soar.

—Hsien Seow

To my dad who raised me with the spirit of innovation, to my family that has nurtured me with love, and to my husband and children who give my life purpose and happiness.　　　　—Sue Tan Toyofuku

THE VOICES BEHIND THIS BOOK

This is not your typical business book. It is a family project inspired by the life teachings of Teng-Kee Tan, PhD, former dean and Harzfeld Professor of Technology Entrepreneurship and Innovation of the Henry W. Bloch School of Management, University of Missouri, Kansas City, and co-authored by his nephew Hsien Seow, PhD, and his daughter, Sue Tan Toyofuku, MSc. Each of them was grappling with their own challenges to bring about innovation and positive change in their respective careers as teachers, consultants, and researchers. As they pursued their lives independently in different countries and fields, they eventually found themselves walking together on the path of innovation. They combined forces and began learning from one another, especially how to teach innovation to others. Over several years, they created this book to help you navigate the complex world of innovation and realize your innovation dream.

TENG-KEE TAN

I am a businessman-turned-academic, teaching entrepreneurship and innovation to others and helping them to successfully innovate in business and reach their innovation dreams. I have been a practitioner and teacher of innovation and management principles for nearly four decades. As a professor, I realized that much of the curriculum taught in traditional business schools was too abstract for many entrepreneurs and innovators in the field. But there is a debate about whether you can actually teach entrepreneurship and innovation, and whether it is a science or an art. My experience, gained from teaching thousands of students all over the world, is that it absolutely can be taught successfully! I've found that it is most effective to teach innovation using a learn-by-doing or experiential learning pedagogy, so that students can apply the knowledge to their own real-world situations right away. Therefore, innovation is *both* a science and an art. Co-writing this book involved systematically documenting and compiling my lifetime of experience and teaching materials, and then refining it into a holistic book about the way of innovation.

HSIEN SEOW

I am an academic researcher that generates evidence that can be used to transform the health care system for the better. Yet, I often struggle with the disconnect between research evidence and policy and practice change. I get frustrated with the inertia of change within the current system and the ineffectiveness of incremental change. Moreover, the pace of generating and publishing research evidence is slow, whereas technologies, treatments, and market forces influencing the delivery of care change quickly. Co-writing this book was an opportunity to explore health care as a business and how businesses innovate, specifically how they create whole-system innovation within an industry. I applied my writing skills as an academic and my teaching skills as a professor to help make the book a useful learning experience for the reader. This book is inspired by my desire to generate knowledge that can be a bridge between scientific evidence and system change, and be applied immediately to help support real-world change.

SUE TAN TOYOFUKU

I am a designer and innovation consultant turned start-up executive, who is passionate about how products, services, and processes can better serve people and improve lives. I strongly believe that innovation is a creative process. Having consulted for a diverse range of organizations around the world, tackling varied complex business and social challenges, my expertise lies in unearthing user insight, challenging assumptions to think outside the box, and designing new concepts and strategies to help organizations innovate. However as a consultant, I became keenly aware that much of our work rarely made it all the way through to implementation and if it did, the final result was usually quite a departure from the original design intent. Co-writing this book was an opportunity to help understand how the creative process and "design thinking" (which I write about in Chapter 4) can be integrated with strategic business practices to meld the art and science of innovation. As a designer, I was also the champion of the reader's experience, wanting the book's layout and design to be engaging and innovative in its approach to how we told our story. This book is inspired by my desire to help people to see the value of a multi-dimensional approach to innovation: an approach that values the philosophical, creative, curious, strategic, and optimistic side of all of us.

3950

PREFACE

This book represents the culmination of more than 40 years of practicing, sharing, teaching, and living innovation. It is quite literally my life's learning on innovation.

I have more than 27 years of experience as a senior corporate executive and entrepreneur in connection with two global ventures, during which I lived and breathed the many innovation management principles and corporate change and transformation strategies that are followed in the real world. After earning a Bachelor of Commerce degree in industrial management from Nanyang University, Singapore, I went on to work in corporate America and Europe, spending 18 years as a senior executive in large global corporations (Electrolux AB and Sunbeam Corporation). Early in my corporate career, I received my MBA from the Kellogg School of Management at Northwestern University. During those nearly two decades, I practiced and implemented innovation in large global organizations quite successfully. I introduced and sustained more than 700 new consumer products and won a few business awards along the way. I eventually left corporate America to start my own business in the late 1980s and spent the next nine years founding and operating two international global ventures in new product design, development, and manufacturing. During those 27 years as a senior corporate executive and entrepreneur, I confronted the most critical challenges facing innovators today. I know what it means to sit in front of a board of directors and defend your strategic plan, ask investors for money, convince partners to share risk, invest your own capital, and risk everything to test your convictions and for what you believe in. I understand what matters most in innovation.

In 1999, at the age of 48, I left the business world to follow my other life-long passion: education. I was given the opportunity to teach entrepreneurship and innovation at my alma mater, which is now named Nanyang Technological University, Singapore. The university was wholly founded and funded by the common people of Singapore who were then under British colonial rule. Its mission was to educate overseas Chinese citizens in their mother tongue, Mandarin, a language that British colonial rulers did not acknowledge. Nonetheless, taxi drivers, hard laborers, trishaw riders, and even cabaret dancers gave their hard-earned money and savings to help fund this private university. Nanyang University was the first Chinese university to be founded outside China. It instilled in me the mantra that ordinary people could do extraordinary things.

While teaching at Nanyang, I obtained my PhD from the Judge Institute of Management Studies, Cambridge University, at the "late" age of 52, focusing on technology, innovation, and entrepreneurship. I have more than 15 years of experience teaching innovation and entrepreneurship around the world. Along the way, I have created and led programs for entrepreneurship and innovation that have received national and international recognition. I am the founding director of and champion for the Technopreneurship and Innovation Program, Nanyang Technological University, which has won international acclaim for its unique experiential approach to instilling the skills and mindset of entrepreneurship. I also become the dean of the Henry W. Bloch School of Management at the University of Missouri, Kansas City, in 2009. As dean for five years, I applied the Tao of Innovation practices in this book to work with the institution and broader community to implement innovation strategies and to help the Bloch School become a national model and global leader in innovation education—proof that running a business school is, in many ways, similar to running a business venture. Because of the innovation change strategy we embarked on as a university community, combined with the top research scholars at the institution and our students' success, the Bloch School has become, in the last four years, a top-tier management school for entrepreneurship and innovation. Its Regnier Institute for Entrepreneurship and Innovation has created undergraduate and graduate programs that have been recognized as the National Model for Entrepreneurship & Innovation Programs by the United States Small Business and Entrepreneurship Association.

However, it is not the accolades from the educational programs I helped build that inspired this book, but rather my experience teaching innovation strategy to thousands of students from all over the globe during the past 15 years. Through my teaching, I realized that innovators across the world ask the same questions and face the same dilemmas. Generally, I identified nine questions every innovator asks along the journey of innovation. Hence I wrote this book to answer these questions and help others to do so too. I realized that my many decades of experience and insights as an entrepreneur gave me the ability to identify the most pertinent innovation and management strategies that could help solve those nine dilemmas. Inspired by my Chinese cultural roots, I use the eight natural elements (fire, earth, wind, water, etc.) from the Taoist compass (called the Bagua) plus the yin-yang to serve as a framework and metaphorically answer the nine questions. This is why the book's title, *The Tao of Innovation*, is appropriate; Tao means "the way" in Chinese. Thus, the Tao of Innovation shows you "the way" of innovation—how and why it occurs. This book is written for all people, from any background, who aspire to be innovators and agents of change. It is also appropriate for use in any type of enterprise, organization, or industry. The book goes beyond an examination of innovative products and services; it focuses on how to create game-changing innovation in an entire industry or business management system.

The Tao of Innovation contributes to the innovation and entrepreneurship knowledge base in five unique ways. First, most innovation books delve deeply into a particular theory, but no one theory can explain every phenomenon or solve every business problem. This book synthesizes multiple theories into a practical framework to serve as a roadmap for innovation. Second, unlike most other books on innovation, this one addresses the complexities of real-world implementation and how to overcome organizational resistance to change, which are often the biggest stumbling blocks to innovation, especially for large organizations. Third, this book is also intended to help you develop an immediate action plan. Each chapter contains tools and exercises to help you answer the nine key questions and create a strategy to implement real change right away. Fourth, the book's very design is innovative and visual. The layout and graphics will help you grasp complex concepts quickly, perform educational exercises, and thus, learn by doing. Fifth, and perhaps most important, this book was deliberately conceived to help ordinary people do extraordinary things. I want to help those who aspire to build a better world to learn how to achieve that goal. I wrote this book to inspire others to innovate purposefully so as to transform an industry or system but also to advance society and human civilization.

Here, I would like to briefly acknowledge my co-authors: my daughter, Sue Tan Toyofuku, who spent several years as a design researcher and innovation consultant for IDEO, the world's leading innovation and design firm, and my nephew, Dr. Hsien Seow, an associate professor and a top health care researcher at Canada's McMaster University. In the process of collaborating to overcome the challenges they faced in implementing innovation in their respective careers, we decided to write this book. This family project is a true equal collaboration of all three authors, though we felt it simplest to tell the story of innovation from my perspective in the first person.

Ultimately, this book is about helping you to achieve your innovation dream, which should focus on developing a deep purpose in life and help you to figure out how to make a positive impact on the world.

Sincerely,
Teng-Kee Tan

This book is an action plan to help you develop a strategy to achieve your innovation dream.

action plan

In Chinese philosophy, the Tao (Chinese character 道) represents "the way" to finding harmony with the underlying natural order of the universe. The Tao is symbolized by elements in nature that are interconnected through a dynamic balance. This book is about "The Way of Innovation." The forces and elements of innovation are as complex as those found in nature; yet we must find a path forward when we want to create change. Based on 40 years of business experience and teaching, this book presents an action plan for innovators, walking them through nine key questions to reflect on and answer. These questions pave the way toward using fundamental practices to help increase your chances of achieving successful innovation.

develop a strategy

Each chapter in this book describes tools and critical practices to help you answer the nine key questions to overcome the innovation challenges you face. Because these questions holistically address the fundamental practices of successful innovation, from inspiration to implementation, they will give you a useful strategy that you can apply to the real demands of your organization, customers, investors, and your market. While I help you ask the right questions, I also provide useful, actionable innovation practices.

innovation dream

I believe that aspiring to innovate is having a dream to change the way something is currently being done. While there are many types of innovation, this book is about making a big picture change and positive impact, not incremental improvements or temporary spikes in efficiency and profits (although those are important too). I address not only business considerations, but also the heart and mind, which must work in concert to successfully innovate. It is my mission to help you find a path to realizing your innovation dream.

THIS BOOK'S FOCUS IS ON GAME-CHANGING INNOVATION

Innovation is essentially about solving problems and changing things for the better. Contrary to popular belief, often innovation is not about inventing new-to-the-world ideas, but about taking existing elements and discovering novel ways of combining and improving them.

The aim and impact of innovation can range from incremental to shifting paradigms. We live in a fiercely competitive and rapidly changing economic, social, and technology landscape. Many organizations are fighting just to stay afloat, defend their market share, or find a slight edge over the competition. Finding incremental ways to improve a product, service, process, or system is sometimes necessary and requires innovative thinking, but the world's problems are increasingly complex and require game-changing ideas to make a real difference and shift away from outdated and ineffective models. The reality is that game-changing innovation is a herculean feat, with high risks, a high likelihood of failure, and a great deal of mystery and uncontrollable forces. Few books exist to help people navigate the daunting journey of game-changing innovation from a holistic approach; for that reason I wrote this book to serve as a catalyst for ground-breaking change. It provides a framework and strategies to help innovators change the very structure of a business and create new business models and opportunities. Regardless of the industry or organization in which you work or the professional title you hold, this book is dedicated to helping big-picture dreamers and visionaries who want to shape the future for the better and dare to dream big.

Innovation takes all forms, including:

- designing better products (e.g., more intuitive smartphones);

- providing more user-friendly services and experiences (e.g., more convenient airline planning and travel);

- developing more effective processes (e.g., cleaner refinement of raw materials);

- changing the structure of an organization or system (e.g., more patient-centered health care);

- influencing and shifting people's behaviors (e.g., promoting healthier eating).

This book can be useful to you wherever you may be in your innovation journey:

As a LEARNER

You may not have much real-world experience or business knowledge yet, but you want to get an overview of the best in innovation thinking. This book will give you a broad understanding of the process of innovation and an overarching framework that you can build upon as you learn more about business, management, and innovation.

As a DOER

You are on the front lines, in the trenches, perhaps working on one part of a larger initiative for change, but are struggling with figuring out how to get from "here" to "there." You may aspire to make a significant, positive difference, but are frustrated over your inability to break away from the status quo. This book will help you to resolve some of the key tensions that are inherent in achieving change and innovation. It will help you to determine what steps to take to create value and shape your organization's future.

As an ENABLER

You are leveraging your expertise and resources to influence and help others to achieve their innovation goals but wonder if they are following the best advice. This book will help you apply the most important business strategies and innovation theories, as well as identify and develop game-changing successes so you can become a better investor, mentor, teacher and advisor.

As a LEADER

You are in charge of inspiring and executing your organization's vision and direction, but wonder how to create a strategic plan that will allow your business to thrive in an uncertain future. This book will help you to redefine and reposition your company to increase its chances of innovating, competing, and growing over time.

Do you have an innovation dream?

Each of these innovators had a dream to create positive change...

MARTIN LUTHER KING, JR.
civil rights activist;
INNOVATION: non-violent civil
rights leadership.
Had a dream to change the way
people of color were treated in
America.

ALBERT EINSTEIN
physicist;
INNOVATION: theory of relativity.
Had a dream to change the way
people understood the laws of
physics.

DENG XIAO PENG,
political leader;
INNOVATION: free market economy
with Chinese characteristics.
Had a dream to change the way
China was governed to alleviate
widespread poverty and transform
the country into a developed nation.

STEVE JOBS
CEO of Apple;
INNOVATION: design-driven
technology.
Had a dream to change the way
people experience and interact
with technology.

**FLORENCE
NIGHTINGALE**
pioneering nurse;
INNOVATION: standardized nursing
practices.
Had a dream to change the way
statistics and sanitation methods
were used to save lives.

SUN TZU
author of *The Art of War*;
INNOVATION: modern strategic
warfare.
Had a dream to evolve the way
people engage in conflict and
warfare.

My dream is to change the way… *innovation is learned*

I have spent the last decade as an educator, helping people from different industries, countries, and walks of life to achieve their innovation dream. But before joining academia, I lived and breathed innovation in the real business world beyond an ivory tower. I spent nearly three decades working for the world's largest corporations as a senior executive, and then took the plunge of starting my own global product development ventures. Around the age of 50, after years of toiling in the business world, I decided to answer a life-long call to become an educator and began as a professor of business, marketing, strategy, and innovation, then moved on to become the director and creator of numerous business and innovation programs, and finally had the privilege to serve as the dean of the Henry W. Bloch School of Management at the University of Missouri in Kansas City, which is ranked as the world's number one school for innovation and management research.

As a corporate executive and entrepreneur, my personal triumphs and tribulations taught me a great deal about what actions lead to success or failure. But becoming a teacher and mentor to thousands of students, executives, and entrepreneurs on innovation has allowed me to gain even more exposure to different industries and global markets, and to reflect deeply on what works and what doesn't when it comes to successful real-world innovation. My unique background as a businessman-turned-academic allows me to synthesize the massive amounts of available information on this broad topic to identify the most pertinent theories that are useful for innovators.

Because innovation has long been a buzzword in the business world and beyond, there are shelves full of writings on this topic, ranging from business management, strategy, to innovation books. Having read most of them, I found that business books tend to delve deeply into a single theory or approach but there are a myriad of elements that need to be considered and, in many cases, mastered for success. Yet few of these books explain how to bring the disparate puzzle pieces together. Knowing how to combine and apply all the fragmented concepts is my students' greatest challenge; as a result, my teaching has always been focused on helping people navigate the entire cycle of innovation. Ultimately I realized that there are common challenges that every innovator faces throughout this journey, regardless of the industry in which they work. I have worked hard to synthesize these common challenges, filter the overwhelming body of theories, models, books, and articles, and tap into my own personal experience and philosophy to craft useful teaching materials and lectures that help people ask the right questions and to discover the answers.

This book is the culmination of all the experience and discoveries I have shared with the thousands of students I have taught around the world. I have tested and refined these precepts based on what my students have reported as proven to work. This book presents the most practical and powerful practices they have successfully used to overcome their day-to-day challenges once they leave the comfort of the lecture room.

The knowledge presented here is bolstered by the diverse expertise and experience of my co-authors, Hsien Seow, PhD, a health care researcher who seeks to bridge research and policymaking to move beyond incremental change in complex health care systems around the world, and Sue Tan Toyofuku, MSc, a design and innovation strategist and who spent seven years working for IDEO, the world's leading innovation and design firm, where she worked with global clients to solve complex problems through a human-centered lens.

What is *your* innovation dream?

Have a good think and fill in the next page.

I always ask my students
to complete this sentence
for themselves:

I have a dream to change the way...

HERE ARE THE NINE KEY QUESTIONS THAT ALL INNOVATORS MUST ASK AND ANSWER ALONG THE JOURNEY OF CREATING AND SUSTAINING CHANGE:

Realizing your innovation dream is not easy. Innovation is never a straight line. But the *Tao of Innovation* will help you navigate the journey. In this book, I have addressed the holistic process of innovation, from vision to implementation, and distilled the most important principles into a series of nine strategic questions and practices. The nine questions will help you to identify and focus on the essential issues; and the associated practices will give you action steps you can use to find the answers.

How is the nature of your business going to change?

Even the most successful innovations have a shelf life and can quickly become obsolete when market dynamics and consumer values shift. While major shifts may pose a threat to your existing business, the opportunity to innovate arises precisely when those with foresight sense change on the horizon. The answer to this question lies in the practice of **constructing a View of the Future**.

How do you know when there is an opportunity for innovation?

Before you develop and launch an innovation you need to understand the forces that affect you. These may be technological, competitive, economic, social, and/or political in nature. These forces are never static and need to be assessed continuously to ensure that you understand the context in which you are operating. The answer to this question lies in the practice of **scanning your environment**.

How do you compete to outsmart established players?

Eighty percent of new businesses fail within the first year. If you take a step back and study innovators who have managed to beat the odds, you can learn from the strategies they employed that increase your likelihood of gaining traction and succeeding in the market. The answer to this question lies in the practice of **crafting a smart innovation strategy**.

How do you move beyond the status quo?

Most organization owners and managers aspire to be innovative and think outside the box; yet, when it comes to developing ideas and solutions, many resist deviating from their standard operating procedures and any challenges to the status quo. You need to enable creative thinking and experimentation that can lead to promising market opportunities and uncover customers' unarticulated needs. The answer to this question lies in the practice of **inspiring breakthrough ideas**.

5 — **How do you put yourself in the right place at the right time?**

Success is not accidental; it is driven by changing market forces and other developments. If you introduce your innovation in the absence of a driving market force, it will fail. You need to time the roll out of your innovation to ensure that it rides the headwinds of profit and consumer adoption. The answer to this question lies in the practice of **riding the waves of opportunity**.

6 — **How do you craft a strong and lasting go-to-market strategy?**

To succeed in business, you need a solid go-to-market master plan to roll out your venture or idea. Your business master plan serves as a blueprint for how you intend to get your offering to your user and trigger adoption and wealth. This master plan needs to be carefully but adaptively conceived and implemented to reduce the risk of failure and sustain your competitive advantage in the appropriate market. The answer to this question lies in the practice of **building a master plan**.

7 — **How do you know whether your idea can survive in the real world?**

While a great deal of ingenuity and thinking has gone into your business idea, what you assume will happen when you enter the market may not occur; the future is unpredictable. There are no guarantees but there are ways to make your business plan more foolproof and test how your plan will withstand consumer, competitive, and market forces. The answer to this question lies in the practice of **passing the stress test**.

8 — **How do you scale successfully?**

Most ventures fail during the process of scaling the innovation; yet the ability to scale is key to growing a sustainable business. The skills that helped to launch an innovation are not the type of expertise required for scaling and taking a start-up to the next level. To succeed in the long term, many informal or improvised ways of working need to transition into effective attitudes, people, and processes to avoid pitfalls in execution. The answer to this question lies in the practice of **preparing for rapid growth**.

9 — **What drives you to innovate?**

Innovation is difficult and may take years to bear fruit. Having a deeper purpose and passion to improve the world in some way is often necessary to stick with it throughout the highs and lows. This answer to this question lies in the practice of **sustaining with purpose**.

IF THESE ARE THE RIGHT QUESTIONS, HOW DOES THIS BOOK HELP YOU ANSWER THEM?

Like most things in life, finding the answers to these nine fundamental questions will require a great deal of personal reflection and hard work on your part. With the infinite number of differences in each market, industry, organization, and among readers, there can be no effective, one-size-fits-all answer. But what I have discovered is a common approach to finding the answers, which I present in this book. *The Tao of Innovation* is about arming yourself with the right frame of mind, tools, and practices to be able to face the tough challenges that come with innovating, and more importantly, to know when and where in the iterative process to employ them. The nine questions and practices of *The Tao of Innovation* collectively pave the way toward the answers.

The Tao is a perfect metaphor for innovation.

As human beings, we tend to learn, understand, and remember most effectively through metaphors. Business, strategy, and innovation are fraught with such complexity that it is easy to become overwhelmed by all the details. As a teacher, I always challenge myself to tell a simple story so people can walk away with what is important. Having been born and raised in Asia, I grew up learning about Taoism and how its teachings are ingrained in the Chinese culture. Although I am not a practicing Taoist, I have always felt a strong connection with its dynamic perspective on how natural and human forces are intertwined, how to reconcile opposing values to achieve harmony, the integration of philosophy and action, and the mystical and practical. It was not until I sat down to write this book with my co-authors, and we struggled to tell a simpler story, that the Tao emerged as an ideal metaphor. Upon deeper reflection, the fundamental principles of Taoism represented the key practices of successful innovation in a very poetic and meaningful way.

In Chinese, Tao means "the way." As the core philosophy of Taoism, it represents the flow that keeps the natural order of the universe in balance. Taoism centers on the cyclical continuity and complexity of the natural world, and its contrast to the linear, goal-oriented actions of human beings. Tao is a beautiful metaphor for innovation because innovation is not a straight line, but a virtuous cycle. Tao, and the pursuit of it, is often represented by the symbol of an eight-sided Taoist compass, called a Bagua (八卦) in Chinese. This compass is used to predict natural events and inform ways to find balance in our lives and environments amid the constantly changing forces of the universe around us.

In this book, we use the eight elements plus the yin-yang of the Tao to symbolize the nine essential questions and related practices in the cycle of innovation. These collectively form "the way" to find the answers to the nine questions every innovator must answer.

The Bagua is composed of eight natural elements that surround the yin-yang: fire, earth, marsh, heaven, water, mountain, thunder, and wind. Taoists believe that these are the basic elemental forces that exist in all forms of life. While each element possesses a different energy and serves a difference purpose in nature, they are arranged in an octagon to symbolize their interdependence. I use the unique properties and characteristics of the elements as inspiration for the essence of each key innovation question and corresponding innovation practice.

The yin-yang is at the center of the Bagua. The yin-yang represents the dynamic balance of contrary forces such as shadow/light, male/female, positive/negative, that are interconnected and interdependent in the natural world. To Taoists, maintaining this dynamic balance and harmony between the forces that are in tension lies at the heart of the philosophy. The yin-yang shows that tensions do not have to be in conflict but can be complementary and synthesized to form a whole that is greater than the sum of its parts. It is the heart of the Bagua and, therefore, is central to understanding the dynamics of innovation.

The deeper the tension an innovation can resolve, the better the chance of its success. Business innovation (and life for that matter) is also about resolving tensions and dilemmas and finding opportunities, whether among the market forces in an industry or in any day-to-day occurrences. As a result, I combine each key innovation question and practice with the inherent tensions and conflicting values you will face as you try to answer and act upon them. At the end of each chapter, I discuss the central real-world tension in that particular innovation practice that you will need to resolve in your organization and even within your own mind as you move forward.

How is the nature of your business going to change?
FIRE
火
How do you scale successfully?
WIND
风
How do you know when there is opportunity for innovation?
EARTH
地
YIN-YANG
What is the deeper purpose that drives you to innovate?
阴阳
How do you know whether your idea can survive in the real world?
THUNDER
雷
How do you compete to outsmart established players?
MARSH
泽
MOUNTAIN
山
HEAVEN
天
WATER
水
How do you craft a strong and lasting go-to-market strategy?
How do you move beyond the status quo?
How do you put yourself in the right place at the right time?

EACH CHAPTER CONTAINS THE FOLLOWING COMPONENTS:

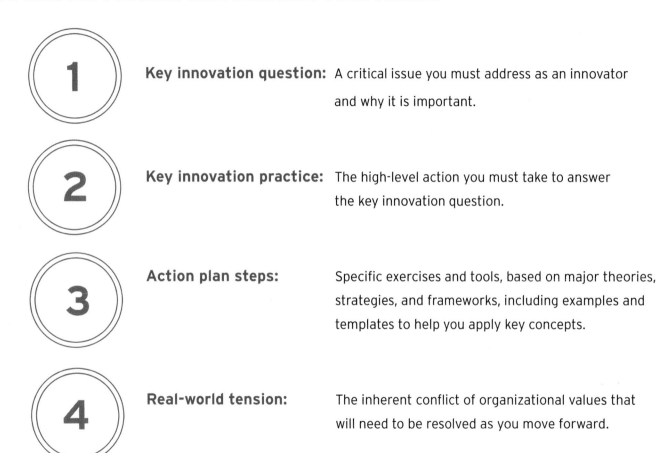

1   **Key innovation question:** A critical issue you must address as an innovator and why it is important.

2   **Key innovation practice:** The high-level action you must take to answer the key innovation question.

3   **Action plan steps:** Specific exercises and tools, based on major theories, strategies, and frameworks, including examples and templates to help you apply key concepts.

4   **Real-world tension:** The inherent conflict of organizational values that will need to be resolved as you move forward.

Applying the Tao principles and practices to your business will allow you to develop a customized strategy and action plan to achieve your innovation dream.

TABLE OF CONTENTS

How is the nature of your business going to change?

Fire symbolizes "the way"
to answer this question.

Fire ILLUMINATES. Fire is energy
and light. This element enables us
to illuminate the forces, trends,
and market shifts that will shape
the future.

Fire represents the practice of
Constructing a View of the Future.

How is the nature of your business going to change?

WHY IS THIS QUESTION IMPORTANT?

Even the most successful innovations have a shelf life and can quickly become obsolete when market dynamics and consumer values shift. If your business is a start-up, it is equally important to create offerings that anticipate future needs. While major market shifts may pose a threat to an existing business, they also represent an opportunity to innovate for those with foresight to sense and capitalize on emerging and significant changes on the horizon.

efore you take any steps along the journey of innovation you have to ask yourself: "What market forces will compel my organization or business to change in the future?" If any exist, you will need to innovate. But do you really believe in the need to change?

Innovation *is* change. In fact, the statement, "The only constant is change," attributed to the Greek philosopher Heraclitus, is true from my experience. But do you believe that your organization needs to embark on a process of change and innovation to stay ahead of changing market forces? Do you think that, in the future, your organization will survive or, better yet, thrive? Will you lead the pack or follow it? Ultimately, do you have a sense of urgency about the need for change?

This chapter is about figuring out where and in what direction your organization should go. It may continue in the direction you are heading today or the path may diverge radically. If you are unsure, then the concepts and tools in this chapter will help you determine whether you need to change and innovate. If you already feel pressure to do things differently, this chapter will provide you with a way to determine where to start on this journey. It will also help you create a shared sense of urgency among those you work with to make positive changes to your organization. Creating a shared sense of urgency to embark on big-scale change is the most important but most difficult hurdle to overcome.

STEPS FOR YOUR ACTION PLAN	WHAT THEY HELP YOU ACCOMPLISH
Construct a View of the Future	Helps you to predict future trends and needs so that your organization can anticipate and capitalize on them as they emerge
Lay new bets	Directs your organization's structure, resource allocation, capability development, and ultimately its innovation strategy
Revise your mission and vision	Aligns your organization's purpose and aspirations with the new bets you have laid about the future to drive change

CONSTRUCTING A VIEW OF THE FUTURE

To help answer this chapter's key innovation question, I am inspired by the writings of Gary Hamel and C. K. Prahalad in their book, *Competing for the Future* (1994), hailed as one of the best business books of the year by *BusinessWeek* magazine. Gary Hamel is a world-renowned management expert and the late C. K. Prahalad was a professor of corporate strategy and a prominent business scholar. In *Competing for the Future*, they point out the need for organizations to develop a "View of the Future," which I strongly believe is the first step to take when embarking on the journey of innovation. The View of the Future consists of hypotheses about how various aspects of your business will change over the next two decades, informed by your foresight about possible future trends and driving forces. Your View of the Future answers critical questions about where the industry is headed with respect to its changing customer priorities, forces affecting the market (e.g., technological, governmental, legal, social, and economic), customer profiles, and competition, all of which can result in a shift in profit mix, supplier mix, and distribution channel mix. In essence, it is about analyzing the possible "state of change" in the ecosystem of an industry. This View of the Future will serve as a guidepost and form the core of your innovation strategy, ranging from how you build new capabilities and resources to how you evolve your mission and vision. Creating a View of the Future requires foresight which comes from having deep insights into industry trends in technology, customer behavior and lifestyle change, regulations, and competitive behavior. These changes can redraw conventional industry boundaries and create new games and rules in new market spaces.

When you construct a View of the Future, you make an educated prediction about fundamental questions:

→ How will the future of your industry be different from today?

→ How will you shape your organization to take advantage of the future changes?

→ How will you change the way you organize your business to compete and satisfy customer needs in the future?

→ What capabilities must you start to build now to become a leader in your industry?

Specifically, you can think about key parts of your business and ask:

- What are customers' priorities today and how will they change in the future?

- Which customers do I serve today and how will they change in the future?

- What channels do I use to reach them today and which ones will I use down the road?

- Who are my competitors today and who will they be in the future?

- What is the basis for my competitive advantage today and what will it be in the future?

- Where do my margins come from today and where will they come from in the future?

- What are our core competencies today and what new capabilities and core competencies do we need to develop to compete in the future?

There are probably other key components and outside forces that are relevant to your business which may change over time. On the next page is a helpful tool to systematically conduct your View of the Future analysis.

Introducing the View of the Future Fan

The View of the Future fan, shown below, is a useful tool because it helps you visualize, summarize, and structure your analysis of future trends. The generic View of the Future lists a summary of different forces that might affect your industry and business. To use the fan effectively, you should consider each of the forces' impact on the past, present, and future. Most importantly, the View of the Future will help you to systematically identify trends that have the potential to be significantly game-changing (not incremental trends that will have a small impact on your business), and would fundamentally alter the way you operate your business today if they transpired.

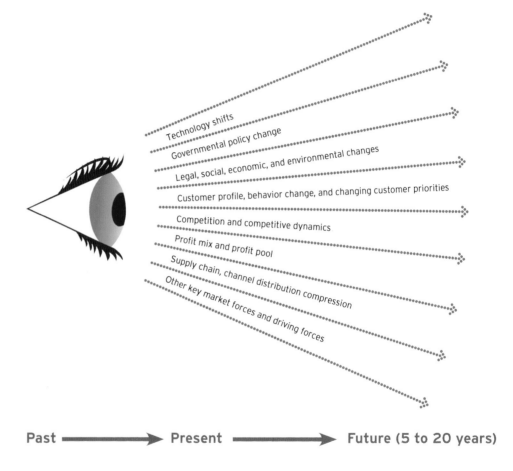

Technology shifts

Governmental policy change

Legal, social, economic, and environmental changes

Customer profile, behavior change, and changing customer priorities

Competition and competitive dynamics

Profit mix and profit pool

Supply chain, channel distribution compression

Other key market forces and driving forces

Past ➝ Present ➝ Future (5 to 20 years)

LAYING NEW BETS

In your View of the Future, you have identified the significant trends and market forces that could have major impacts on your industry. Now you can proceed to lay your bets about to what extent and how the future will be different from the way it is today. Laying your bets involves choosing big bets that will lead to a fundamental shift in the way you organize your business to compete in the future.

It is called a bet because there is no guarantee about how the future will unfold. Making bets are uncertain and sometimes risky but you need to make informed decisions based on market trends, forces driving the market, market intelligence, and changing customer priorities and values. Most importantly, you need to follow through and align your organization to the bets you're making.

Your bets serve as a pivot to help you transform your current business model, the manner in which you deliver your product or service, or the type of customer you are serving. You might realize that what is generating profit today may not be your key profit driver in the next 5 to 10 years. You will, therefore, need to examine your product mix and distribution model and think of how you might reinvent your organization to meet the needs of the future you have predicted.

Why Lay New Bets?
If you don't lay new bets when the future trend is changing dramatically, you risk running your business the same way or changing incrementally and then becoming obsolete. Meanwhile competitors with new bets will invent new games and new rules that will govern the market. They will also have first-mover advantage and will have locked up strategic relationships with the best first-tier suppliers in the industry. Gary Hamel believes that "competing for the future" is about rule making, innovation and growth, and repositioning your strategy and core capabilities. It is about having foresight about the future and behaving more like an architect who is trying to design the future rather than a process engineer who is trying to improve the company's efficiency in a status quo environment. While there is no guarantee that your bets will be correct, merely waiting to see what happens before putting any stakes in the ground will result in "too little too late." Those who have the guts and foresight to make the right bets will be in an advantageous position to strike first.

Making Big Bets is Fundamental to Game-changing Innovation

What qualifies as a big bet? A useful metaphor to identify which bets will have a game-changing and fundamental impact on your industry and business is to use the 80/20 ➜ 20/80 rule. Applied here, it is based on the premise that 80% of your current sales mix or product offering today might be reduced to only 20% in the future; the big bets are the ones that have the potential to cause that kind of flip. Big bets also mean big profit opportunities.

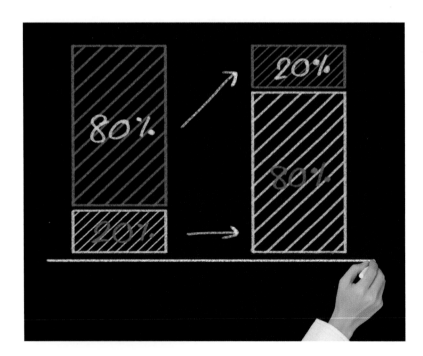

The following are examples of industries that went through this metaphorical 80/20 → 20/80 flip:

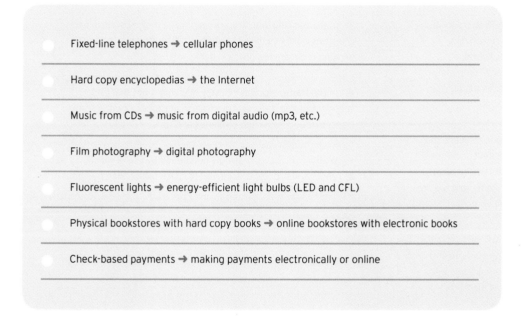

- Fixed-line telephones → cellular phones

- Hard copy encyclopedias → the Internet

- Music from CDs → music from digital audio (mp3, etc.)

- Film photography → digital photography

- Fluorescent lights → energy-efficient light bulbs (LED and CFL)

- Physical bookstores with hard copy books → online bookstores with electronic books

- Check-based payments → making payments electronically or online

These examples serve as cautionary tales to show that even if you are "the 80%" of today, you risk becoming "the 20%" of tomorrow if you don't lay new bets for the future and start to align your organization to meet those needs.

Below are examples of what bets might be realistic in the future in various industries that tend to follow the 80/20 → 20/80 rule.

- In the automobile business, you might bet that 15 years from now, more than 80% of the automobiles sold will run on non-conventional fuel (i.e., natural gas, electric battery, hybrid, etc.); most cars, trucks, boats, and aircraft will be partly or completely self-driven or autonomous; or 50% of the cars will be made from recyclable materials.

- In the grocery business, you may bet that in 10 to 15 years, the governments might ban the sale of high- sugar-content soda in schools, or that advertising of unhealthy soft drinks will be banned. Or you might bet that more than 80% of grocery items sold will be organic or natural food with low sugar and low salt content.

- In 10 to15 years, you may bet that health care will shift from a treatment- and cost-driven system to a wellness, prevention, and evidence-based-medicine, value-based model. All Americans will be insured or a hybrid of free market and socialized medicine will dominate. In 20 years, there will be a cure for cancer.

- In the banking industry, you might bet that most developed countries will be cashless societies in 10 years when, although banking is necessary, physical banks are not.

- In the transportation industry, you might bet that high-speed trains will become America's major mode of inter-state transportation, replacing airplanes and cars.

- Warfare will be increasingly conducted by use of machines, such as robots and drones, or from outer space rather than by human soldiers.

If these bets actually come through, they will generate a lot of opportunities for new businesses and innovation and have a game-changing impact on the affected industries.

Creating a Sense of Urgency

Whatever industry you are in, you will probably identify a few major bets that you are confident will happen and will have a fundamental impact on your business. Ask yourself and your executive team: "Based on how your business is organized today (including the core competencies, resource allocations, organizational design, etc.), will it adequately meet the challenge and compete effectively in the future if those bets come to fruition?"

If the answer is no, this should trigger a sense of urgency and should send a shock wave through your company even if it is currently doing very well. You then need to reorganize the way you compete to meet the needs of the future you have predicted, but with a clear sense of urgency now. The rest of this book will help you create a strategy of how to reorganize your business.

If your company is doing well, it is probably because of decisions and bets made many years ago from which you are now well positioned to benefit from. But as the future continues to change rapidly, the bets laid many years ago may not hold true in the future. If you don't lay new bets and start preparing now, who represents the 80% majority of your customers today may dwindle to only 20% in the not-too-distant future. Ultimately, if you fail to adequately incorporate a View of the Future into your business strategy or if you make the wrong bets, it could mean the demise of your organization's business, or worse, the entire industry itself. So what are the new game-changing bets you are willing to make? In which ones are you prepared to invest the resources of your organization?

Our world is rapidly changing, in large part due to advancements in computing power, digital storage capacity and information technology. The May 2013 issue of *McKinsey Global Institute* cited 12 game-changing technologies that are likely to transform businesses, societies, and the global economy in major ways. These technologies are estimated to generate trillions of dollars' worth of economic impact in the global market. They are: mobile computing devices, intelligent software systems, the Internet's ability to optimize processes, cloud computing technology, advance robotics, autonomous and near autonomous vehicles, next-generation genomics, energy storage, 3D printing, advanced materials, advanced oil and gas exploration and recovery, and renewable energy. These technologies represent new ways of doing things with less effort, less energy, and more value creation. It will reshuffle industry profit zones and render old business models and past competitive advantages obsolete. Is your industry affected by these huge technological shifts? How will these technologies change the way you organize your business to compete in the near future?

Hamel and Prahalad studied how Electronic Data Systems (EDS) went through the process of crafting a shared View of the Future and laying new bets for their future business. EDS was founded by former presidential candidate and long-time entrepreneur H. Ross Perot in 1962. The company began as a supplier of computer equipment and had skilled personnel to manage the processing of electronic data. For many decades, the company's business model targeted large corporations, such as the insurance company California Blue Cross, to handle backlogged Medicare data processing claims. It also offered long-term contracts even though short-term contracts were the norm. By 1992, EDS had revenues of $8.2 billion. However, in the early 1990s, the company faced several industry challenges that were shrinking its profits. Perot brought together EDS's senior management to develop a shared View of the Future. The EDS executives concluded that sticking with the company's existing business model and strategy would cause the company to become unprofitable. As a result, they came up with three major new "bets" and turned those into strategies to pursue.

INDUSTRY CHALLENGES FROM THE VIEW OF THE FUTURE	BETS LAID	STRATEGIES PURSUED
The number of large, leading-edge, information technology users was shrinking, which led to heavy discounting in long-term contract pricing	There will be a rapid globalization of information sharing	EDS needs to use information technology to span geographical boundaries
The need for desktop computing capability was far outdistancing the need for mainframe computing	People will suffer from information overload	EDS needs to convert data into meaningful information for decision making and strategy formulation
The focus of information networks had changed from the office to the home	People will want individualization and customization of information	EDS needs to present data and information solutions in a customized way for the masses

The Result

The View of the Future and the ensuing bets EDS made helped it to develop a shared view of the industry's future and a future role that was substantially broader and more creative than they had previously held. Under different CEOs throughout the 1990s, EDS began investing in and acquiring e-business technology companies to enable EDS to be competitive in a globalized economy by providing web-based and e-business solutions operations (e.g., call center management and web-based collaborative product design). This helped the company to succeed and grow during the 1990s when many companies were outsourcing information technology functions. Over that decade, EDS's revenue increased threefold to $25 billion in 2000. Its massive growth came from a major organizational business model innovation based on management's View of the Future.

DO IT YOURSELF

STEP 1

Construct a view of the future: Think through your View of the Future to help you spot huge and significant, not incremental, trends that you think will fundamentally alter the way you operate your business today. When constructing your View of the Future and laying new bets, I encourage you to engage different levels of management staff and employees from various departments to complete the exercise together. The exercise is designed to create a shared View of the Future, lay new bets, and to create a sense of urgency for the company's leadership and employees. It can help you to begin to reorganize and transition the business to function the way it will compete in the future.

Here is a blank View of the Future fan for you and/or the executive team in your organization to complete:

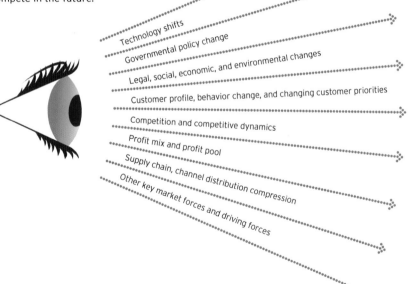

Technology shifts

Governmental policy change

Legal, social, economic, and environmental changes

Customer profile, behavior change, and changing customer priorities

Competition and competitive dynamics

Profit mix and profit pool

Supply chain, channel distribution compression

Other key market forces and driving forces

Past ⟶ Present ⟶ Future (5 to 20 years)

Building on your answers for the View of the Future fan exercise, think through these key questions:

- What are customers' priorities today and how will they change in the future?

- Which customers do I serve today and how will they change in the future?

- What channels do I use to reach them today and which ones will I use down the road?

- Who are my competitors today and who will they be in the future?

- What is the basis for my competitive advantage today and what will it be in the future?

- Where do my margins come from today and where will they come from in the future?

- What are our core competencies today and what new capabilities and core competencies do we need to develop to compete in the future?

NOTE: When you have finished laying your bets you should feel very uncomfortable! This is especially true if you are not ready to succeed and thrive in the future world in which the bets you laid come to fruition. If you do not feel uncomfortable, either you are in an industry that is very stable with no major changes in the forces (e.g., a monopoly that is government controlled) or your bets are too incremental; if the latter is the case, you may want to repeat the View of the Future exercise and read up on the emerging trends.

STEP 2

Lay new bets: Looking at all of the future trends across all the relevant forces, identify a few major bets that will affect your industry or business. The laying of bets will force you to identify which trends are significantly game-changing (i.e., follow the 80/20 ➜ 20/80 metaphor), are likely to happen, and are the ones you should bet on.

REVISING YOUR MISSION AND VISION

After you have laid new bets, it is important to align your organizational resources with your new bets. The best way to do that is to reexamine your current mission and vision statement and change it to reflect and embody your new aspirations. It is similar to climbing a mountain: as you climb higher, the view changes in ways you could not have predicted while you were below. New plateaus provide new vantage points, which inform your plan.

What is a Mission and Vision?

A mission is the organization's reason for being. It is a declaration of the organization's intent. What is the goal and purpose of the organization in the first place? A good mission statement should articulate why a company was created. This provides the framework or context within which the vision, positioning, value proposition, and strategies are crafted, implemented, and operationalized. In contrast, the vision is your dream. What does your organization aspire to become? You may never achieve it, but it is still your vision.

[*Case in Point*] CERNER CORPORATION

Let us look at how Cerner Corporation's vision has evolved over time because of a change in Cerner's View of the Future of the health care industry. Health care has become more complex and inefficient since the 1980s, which was when Cerner started to provide health information technology services to health care providers. Cerner is a 30-year-old health information technology company located in Kansas City, MO. It has revenue of $2.95 billion (2013), a market capitalization of $17.53 billion (July 12, 2014), and approximately 11,000 employees. It sits in the strategic intersection of health care and information technology. The company started by digitizing paper processes but now offers a comprehensive array of medical information software, professional services, medical device integration, remote hosting, and employer health and wellness services. It began as a health information technology company, whose mission was to provide clinical health information to the appropriate providers in the most efficient way.

Hence, its old mission statement was: To connect the appropriate person(s), resource, and knowledge at the appropriate time and location to achieve the optimal health outcome.

Since about 2008, Cerner's top management has been repositioning itself by adopting a broader and more visionary mission and vision. The company's new View of the Future is one of wellness promotion, treatment, and value-based and evidence-based medical care. Cerner believes that health care should revolve around the individual. It no longer sees itself as only a health information technology company, but wants to build on its capabilities in providing electronic medical record technology to help health care providers make better evidence-based medical decisions and ultimately to improve the health and productivity of communities. Cerner Solutions' new strategic direction is to enable organizations to convert health care information technology into intelligence about the health of their populations so they can manage their patients' health, one person at a time, with early interventions. More than 2,700 hospitals, 45,000 physicians, and 10,000 health care facilities globally have purchased Cerner Solutions licenses.

Hence its new mission statement is: To contribute to the systemic improvement of health care delivery and the health of communities.

Let me share a personal example of the impact that a revised mission and vision can have on an organization. When I assumed the position of dean of the Henry W. Bloch School of Business and Public Administration, at the University of Missouri, Kansas City, in 2009, I was responsible for repositioning the school to become a preeminent business school. Using the same key innovation questions this book presents, I began to develop a View of the Future that was shared by the school's stakeholders, including students, alumni, board members, faculty, and administrators across the entire university community.

Our shared View of the Future led to this bet: because globalization is causing employers to seek college graduates who are not only deep in technical competence but also globally competitive, all enterprises (private or public) will want workers who are able to function in cross-disciplinary and cross-cultural settings, with innovative and entrepreneurial mindsets. We bet that employers from all enterprises (public or private) will want a workforce that is globally competitive, can work in diverse teams, and has demonstrated leadership skills in addition to deep technical skills that have long been in demand. This is a big bet because we were previously focused more on producing technically proficient accountants and functional managers with leadership. However, as a result of this bet, we embarked on a process of creating a new strategic plan to reposition

the school from a business and public administration school to a school of management with a focus on entrepreneurship and innovation and entrepreneurial leadership, for both for-profit and nonprofit enterprises.

You can compare the old and new mission statements below to appreciate how an organization's mission statement can change, inspired by a new View of the Future and new bets for an organization.

New Mission Statement

The Henry W. Bloch School of Management develops purposeful, entrepreneurial, and innovative leaders to meet changing global demands, and advances knowledge and practice through teaching, scholarship, outreach, and service. We aspire to be Kansas City's nationally and globally preeminent school of management focusing on entrepreneurial and innovative thinking as the foundation for transforming talent and achieving sustainable growth in for-profit and nonprofit enterprises.

Old Mission Statement

The Henry W. Bloch School of Business and Public Administration supports the mission of the University of Missouri, Kansas City, and provides high-quality professionals with education for a changing world. The school offers undergraduate, graduate, executive, and other outreach programs that are responsive to business and community needs. These programs are delivered through a curriculum combining solid preparation in basic management functions with the skills of leadership, entrepreneurship, strategic decision making, and an understanding of technological and global environment. The school's faculty is committed to teaching, scholarship, and service, and to continuously improving a learning environment that brings discipline to the real-world challenges of management practice.

Chapter 1 thus far highlights the practice of Crafting a View of the Future, which proactively prepares an organization for inevitable changes and shifts in the consumer and competitive landscape. Understanding the action steps is often the easy part. It is more difficult to implement change, particularly when trying to convince others, including senior executives, to fully engage with and support the change and innovation strategy. As any dedicated innovator knows, most people and organizations resist change because they have become comfortable with and tied to the existing ways of doing things, have invested in them, and enjoy the benefits they bring. I have learned that initiating change involves a deep philosophical debate before you can convince yourself or others to undergo the difficult process of innovation.

As you answer this chapter's innovation question, "How is the nature of your business going to change?," be prepared to face tension between the values of:

CONTINUITY VS. **CHANGE**

Continuity is about pragmatism. It is the current culture and the existing way of doing things that pays the bills, feeds the employees, satisfies current customers, and returns dividends to shareholders. Continuity helps your organization stay competitive, profitable, and successful today.

Change is about idealism. It is the result of focusing on a future ideal scenario; about envisioning the future changing in dramatic ways. Your vision of change is shaped by your new aspirations and dreams about serving future customers and needs. But, be warned: the things you seek to change might actually compete with and contradict your organization's current profit-making activities in big ways.

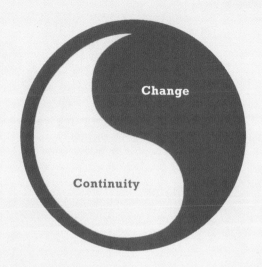

To reconcile the tension between the desire for continuity and the need to change, you need to:

Deliver on today's needs while also shaping tomorrow's future.

Organizations struggle with the fact that they need to change while remaining the same. To resolve this tension, you must not see "change" in opposition to "continuity," but engage in "change and continuity" as a virtuous cycle.

Ironically, businesses and organizations are actually motivated to change by the desire to maintain successful results, such as being profitable and valuable to customers. You may find ways to make changes that slowly move you toward the ideal, while preserving what is precious to you as an organization. If continuity represents "the way we do things now," you need to ask "What way of doing things now can also deliver the improvement we aspire to in the future?" On the other hand, change cannot be completely out of touch with reality. You need to reconcile the real with the ideal to come up with a feasible strategy. You must ask "What continuity do we need to preserve that can facilitate change?"

[*Case in Point*] APPLE

Apple keeps producing its personal computer line of products even though personal computers are not generating the high profits its new product lines, such as the iPod, iPhone, and iPad, are. Apple preserves important continuity in branding and design to continue to appeal to its loyal and captive customer base. The company uses its MacBook line of personal computers as a "product platform" to integrate the functionality of its new generation of iTunes, iPhone, and iPad into a seamless value proposition. This continuity in product platform, branding, and design actually helped Apple to facilitate change and the significant impact its new products have created in the computer industry and our lives.

How is the nature of your business going to change?

Answering this question starts with the practice of:

Constructing a View of the Future

▼ Construct a View of the Future to assess what major shifts you foresee occurring in your industry and/or business in the next 10 years. How different will it look in 10 years?

▼ Based on this View of the Future, lay three new big bets that you believe will become true. Remember that big bets follow the 80/20 ➜ 20/80 metaphor of big change and will, if the bets come true, lead to a major shift in the industry landscape in the next 10 years.

▼ Think about whether your organization is organized to survive and thrive in an environment if these bets were to come to fruition. If it is not, this is the basis for which you develop an urgency for change.

▼ Review and, if necessary, revise your current mission and vision statements to reflect your new bets.

Want to go deeper?

Further Reading

Hamel, G. and Prahalad, C. (1994). *Competing for the future*. Boston, MA: Harvard Business School Press.

Manyika, J., Chui, M., Bughin, R. D., Dobbs, R., Bisson, P., Marrs, A. (2013). *Disruptive technologies: Advances that will transform life, business and the global economy*. Washington, DC: McKinsey Global Institute.

How do you know when there is an opportunity for innovation?

FIRE 火

EARTH 地

WIND 风

YIN-YANG

MARSH 泽

THUNDER 雷

阴阳

MOUNTAIN 艮

HEAVEN 天

WATER 水

Earth symbolizes "the way"
to answer this question.

Earth SURROUNDS you. This
element teaches you to be aware
of the landscape of which you
are a part.

Earth represents the practice of
Scanning Your Environment.

How do you know when there is an opportunity for innovation?

WHY IS THIS QUESTION IMPORTANT?

You wouldn't go sailing without first checking the weather conditions. Similarly, before you launch an innovation you need to understand the existing forces that affect your business, which may be economic, social, and/or political in nature. These forces are never static and need to be continually assessed.

*I*n the previous chapter, you completed the View of the Future exercise, laid new bets, and established "where you want to go." The next step of plotting "how you get there" depends on where your industry is and your position in it. You need to determine the changing forces in your industry's external environment, your organization's current place in the ecosystem, and how those changes might affect you. If you know where your organization stands within the larger ecosystem, you can then assess whether your current resources and capabilities are adequate to meet emerging threats and opportunities.

STEPS FOR YOUR ACTION PLAN	WHAT THEY HELP YOU ACCOMPLISH
Analyze the external environment	Identify the key dynamic changing forces which will fundamentally alter the dynamics of your industry and market
Examine your internal resources and capabilities	Identify needs and opportunities in resource and capability development or acquisitions
Evaluate changing customer priorities	Examine how to capitalize on changes in customer purchasing priorities in the future
Conduct a Strengths-Weaknesses-Opportunities-Threats (SWOT) analysis	Synthesize these analyses to help develop an innovation strategy and sense of urgency

ANALYZING THE EXTERNAL ENVIRONMENT

To assess the state of an industry's innovation potential at both the macro and micro environment, I would like to highlight a set of tools invented by Michael Porter, an acclaimed Harvard Business School professor. Porter is a leading authority on competitive strategy and one of the most cited authors in business and economics. The tools he developed are very useful in helping you to assess the broader industry's structural dynamics and how it might present an opportunity or threat to your organization.

PEST Analysis

This tool is used to examine the **macro environment** to identify changes in the industry's external environment; specifically Political-legal, Economic, Social and Technological factors, summarized as "PEST."

Five Forces

This tool is used to examine the **micro environment** within your industry to assess the level of urgency for change. It considers the most critical five forces that shape the competitive dynamics of your industry: (1) threats to new entrants, (2) intensity of rivalry between industry players, (3) bargaining power of the supplier, (4) bargaining power with your customer, and (5) substitution.

Together, these tools help you think through the external factors that will have a significant impact (both positive and negative) on current and future market dynamics that your industry faces. They also help you to assess whether the predicted changes will make it more attractive or less attractive for you to remain in your industry.

PEST ANALYSIS

The macro PEST factors are external forces that will always have a major effect on your industry and can sometimes create opportunities or threats for competing players.

FACTOR	EXPLANATION	EXAMPLE TREND	INDUSTRIES AFFECTED
Political	What are existing or forthcoming government legislation, regulations, and policies that make the industry more or less attractive and profitable?	Changing bank laws that affect lending	Housing, banking, mortgage brokers, and other financial institutions
Economic	What is the current condition of the economy and what economic trends will affect your industry?	High unemployment rate, slow GDP growth	Social assistance programs, housing, restauranteurs, mortgage lending
Social	What social factors affect your industry?	Aging population, diet trends, popular culture, social media	Medical, health and wellness, information technology, e-commerce communications and entertainment, smartphones and computers
Technology	How do existing and emerging technologies make the industry more or less advantageous for profitability?	Electronic records, cloud computing	Health care providers and hospitals, electronic medical record technology companies, smartphones and communication, social media and e-commerce

FIVE FORCES ANALYSIS

FORCE	EXPLANATION
1. Threats to new entrants	**Has the entry barrier been lowered or raised for potential new players to enter the market?** • A low barrier to entry means it is easier for competition to enter the market. This will intensify the competition and make the industry less attractive by eroding profit margins. Low barriers include low capital investment, low levels of technology required, and little regulation • A high barrier to entry means it is more difficult to enter the market. These include high capital investment costs, requiring respect for patent rights, license purchases, or heavy regulation compliance
2. Intensity of rivalry between industry players	**What is the level of rivalry between competitors?** • If the intensity of rivalry between industry players is very high, it will make the industry less profitable because as the competition becomes more intense, the organizations in the industry will probably have to lower prices to attract more consumers. More competition often benefits consumers with lower prices
3. Bargaining power of the supplier	**What is the extent of the bargaining power of the supplier?** • If the number of suppliers in your industry is large, the suppliers have less bargaining power because the component prices will be low, which in turn is advantageous to the profitability of the industry • Conversely, if the critical components you need are controlled by a few suppliers, this will have a negative impact on the profitability of the industry
4. Bargaining power with consumer	**Who has more power in the relationship between you and your customer?** • When you don't have sufficient bargaining power with your consumers, they can buy from competitors with ease and your profit will be eroded because you cannot charge a premium
5. Substitution	**How easy is it for the consumer to buy another product or service to perform the same function that you offer?** • If the consumer can easily replace your product or service, with a similar product or another one that addresses the same need, then there is a high substitution opportunity and your industry will be negatively impacted

EXAMPLE INDUSTRY

1. Banking (high barrier to entry due to extensive regulation)

   Airline industry (medium barrier to entry due to deregulation, but still requires a lot of capital to buy planes)

   Internet, cloud computing, digital revolution, and open-source operating software system lower the barrier to entry for innovators

2. Gas stations (high rivalry and competition between gas stations, evidenced by very little price difference)

   Smartphone and e-commerce industries have high rivalry between competitors

3. Pharmaceutical "blockbuster" drugs with patents (high bargaining power of the supplier, i.e., the pharmaceutical company)

   Intel's microprocessor commands industry leadership and has limited competition, resulting in little bargaining power for customers

4. Dell sells directly to users with mass-customized features to cut out the middleman. Customers have to pay the listed price for the Dell personal computer features they select

5. The iPad can be used as a personal computer (PC), thus has high substitution ability, which is negative for the PC industry.

   Also the smartphone has increasingly become a mobile computer and can dilute the demand for PCs

The Five Forces that Shape Industry Competition

```
                    ┌─────────────┐
                    │   Threat    │
                    │   of New    │
                    │  Entrants   │
                    └─────────────┘
                           │
                           ▼
                        Rivalry
  ┌─────────────┐       Among        ┌─────────────┐
  │ Bargaining  │ ──▶  Existing  ◀── │ Bargaining  │
  │  Power of   │     Competitors    │  Power of   │
  │  Suppliers  │                    │    Buyers   │
  └─────────────┘                    └─────────────┘
                           ▲
                           │
                    ┌─────────────┐
                    │  Threat of  │
                    │ Substitute  │
                    │ Products or │
                    │  Services   │
                    └─────────────┘
```

Source: From How Competitive Forces Shape Strategy by Michael Porter, *Harvard Business Review.* 57, no. 2 (March-April 1979): 137-145, copyright © 1979. Used with permission of Harvard Business Publishing Corporation.

[*Case in Point*] THE PERSONAL COMPUTER INDUSTRY

Let's examine the significant external environmental changes that the personal computer industry faced in the late 1990s and early 2000s using the PEST analysis.

Political and legal	There have been no major legislative changes to the PC industry
Economic	A macro environment of low interest rates and low labor costs in emerging economies has made it more affordable for consumers to own computers
Social	Positive consumer demographic changes with more people purchasing and using PCs for communication and social media activities
Technological	Technological advances in computing power, cloud capacity, and digital technology have dramatically increased PCs' data storage and processing speed for data, images, and videos

These positive forces helped increase the total demand and usage of PCs in an even more interconnected world via the use of the Internet. However, the positive macro environmental factors of PEST have been seriously negated by the micro environmental five forces. Let's now examine the micro environment using the 5 forces analysis.

Five forces analysis:

The micro environment has become increasingly competitive and less profitable for PC sellers.

Threats to new entrants	There is an ease of entry into the PC manufacturing and marketing industry by emerging economies like China, Korea, and Vietnam, which have relatively low manufacturing cost structures and efficient production methods. Technological advances in computing power speed, cloud computing, and data storage enable innovation and new product development to be carried out at much lower cost and faster speed
Intensity of rivalry between industry players	The new entrants to the market have competition between industry players
Bargaining power of the supplier	The continued dominance of Intel and Microsoft in the microprocessor and operating system markets undercuts the bargaining power of PC makers with their key suppliers
Bargaining power with the consumer	During the 1990s and early 2000s, more than 80% of market capitalization in the PC business was generated by Intel, Microsoft, and Dell. Dell's unique model of selling directly to the consumer, without a middleman, helped increase its profit margin relative to other PC makers such as Lenovo and Hewlett-Packard, which rely heavily on using a go-between, a retail distribution structure, and advertising
Substitution	An increased number of players and the proliferation of feature-loaded smartphones, iPads, tablets, and other alternative handheld devices have reduced the bargaining power of PC makers and further eroded total industry profitability and attractiveness

Companies facing such threats from their environment need to clearly understand which forces are going through dynamic changes and how to reposition their current business models to overcome threats and capitalize on opportunities before their offerings become irrelevant.

Now apply the PEST analysis to your industry.

FACTOR	EXPLANATION	
Political and Legal	What are existing or forthcoming government legislation, regulations and policies that make the industry more or less attractive and profitable?	_____ _____ _____ _____ _____
Economic	What is the current condition of the economy and what economic trends will affect your industry?	_____ _____ _____ _____ _____
Social	What social factors affect your industry?	_____ _____ _____ _____ _____
Technological	How do existing and emerging technologies make the industry more or less advantageous for profitability?	_____ _____ _____ _____

Now apply the five forces analysis to your industry.

FORCE	EXPLANATION	
1. Threats to new entrants	Has the entry barrier been lowered or raised for potential new players to enter the market?	
2. Intensity of rivalry between industry players	What is the level of rivalry between competitors?	
3. Bargaining power of the supplier	What is the extent of the bargaining power of the supplier?	
4. Bargaining power with consumer	What is the extent of the bargaining power of the consumer?	
5. Threat of Substitution	How easy is it for the consumer to buy another product or service to perform the same function that you offer?	

HOW URGENTLY DO I NEED TO INNOVATE?

Imagine your organization as a five-legged stool, with each leg representing one of the five forces.

If no forces are against you, you are sitting pretty; your business model is not being threatened. Your position is very stable. For example, industrial air supply companies such as Air Liquide, British Oxygen Company, and Praxair compete in a very stable industry where the five forces are very stable with few threats and a steady stream of industry profits for all three of the world's major players in this industry.

If just one force is against you, you still have four legs of the stool, which makes your company quite stable, although you can still start to contemplate your innovation strategy.

If two forces are against you, your stool has only three legs and is beginning to become unstable. You need to start seriously thinking about your innovation strategy.

If three or more forces are against you, your stool—your company's competitive platform—is not stable. Your business model is in serious jeopardy and you need to start to implement your innovation strategy immediately. For instance, as mentioned above, the PC industry is typical of one in which most forces are against all the players resulting in very unattractive industry profits. Although Dell, with its direct selling model, is the most profitable among all PC industry players, it recently went private to reposition itself in response to declining returns and profitability. Other major players, such as Hewlett-Packard and Lenovo, continue to suffer from slim profits and continuous margin erosion. Sony recently announced its exit from the PC business and the industry as a whole suffers from negative profits.

INTERNAL ENVIRONMENTAL ANALYSIS:
LOOKING AT RESOURCE AND CAPABILITY GAPS

After you have identified how changes in the external industry might affect your business model, you are ready to examine your organization internally. The resources and capabilities of an organization are bundled together to form what is called your entity's internal value chain. The value chain is a chain of activities that an organization performs in order to deliver a valuable product or service to its customer (such as research and development, manufacturing, marketing and sales, and services). These activities and organizational functions are also supported by activities in human resources, materials management, and the company's strategy and culture.

When evaluating your resources and capabilities, you should consider both tangible and intangible assets that your value chain has to offer. For example, company culture can play just as important a role as does your intellectual property and proprietary technology or efficient manufacturing processes. You should also assess whether there are any that are under-utilized or under-exploited to help serve customers' unarticulated needs. One example is the aforementioned health information technology company, Cerner Corporation, which has expanded its capabilities from digitizing paper-based information to establishing additional health care information technology solutions. These services include remote hosting, application management services, operational management services, and disaster recovery. It has leveraged its internal assets of using information technology to optimize paper processes, such as medical records, to expanding the use of those assets to optimize and integrate multiple health care processes, such as medical devices, pharmacies, documentation, and ordering, thus increasing customer offerings at relatively low cost.

When examining your existing resources and capabilities, the key questions to ask are:

→ Are your organization's current resources and capabilities sufficient to take advantage of potential growth opportunities presented by your external environment?

→ Are your organization's current resources and capabilities adequate to overcome the threats imposed by the external environment?

→ What are your resource and capability gaps?

→ How will you fill these gaps, expand your capability portfolio, and reconfigure your core competencies to meet future growth and innovation opportunities? Is it best to grow them organically through internal development, or acquire them externally through global strategic alliances or mergers and acquisitions? Or can the services you need be outsourced effectively? Perhaps the answer involves a combination of various methods of capability development described here.

New resources and capabilities can be hard to grow internally because they are developed cumulatively and incrementally, based on the needs of existing customers; whereas an innovation often requires dramatically new and different capabilities. Developing capabilities internally not only takes time, but can be problematic for your existing customers, who have much invested in the products and services you provide currently. Most firms acquire new capabilities and resources through mergers and acquisitions to fill gaps that are necessary to exploit new market opportunities. Outsourcing is also an effective way to allow firms to take advantage of components/sub-assemblies or processes that can be produced by specialists with more efficient cost structures to allow firms to focus more on improving their core competencies and activities. Outsourcing makes sense when it increases your overall competitive advantage in aspects that are central to your value proposition—so it benefits your existing customers but also new customers—rather than focusing on those outside your expertise.

Great companies organize their value chain components into unique capabilities and distinctive core competencies to deliver their products and services faster, cheaper, and better. For instance, most companies are capitalizing on the rapid advancement of the Internet, computing power, and cloud computing to aggregate their value chain activities to facilitate "one-to-one customization" and to quickly and flexibly meet each customer's needs. The ability to bundle value chain activities to innovate and bring to market new products and services quickly is another added competitive advantage. The computer chip maker Intel, for example, has proved for many years how its integrated and efficient value chain activities allow it to develop and introduce a new generation of microprocessor chips every 18 months, two years ahead of its competition, which has enabled it to secure a consistently dominant position in the microprocessor business over the last 20 years. They key is to achieve some form of sustainable competitive advantage over the competition that is hard to imitate.

EVALUATING CHANGING CUSTOMER PRIORITIES

Companies roll out their business strategies incrementally, based on the evolution of market forces and customers' priorities. New market forces, such as legislation and regulations—or deregulation—new product/service innovation, and new competitive strategies, can shift customer priorities over time in significant ways. For example, the emergence of healthy and wholesome food companies such as Whole Foods and Trader Joe's in North America that offer customers natural, healthy, organic food that is grown in environmentally sustainable ways has created a whole new generation of health-conscious consumers. These consumers are willing to pay a premium for their food and other products that are healthier, and, in many cases, locally grown, which improves their freshness and are less damaging to the environment to produce and provide. This innovation in the grocery business has shifted the way consumers make buying decisions; many now place a higher priority, not on price and a broad selection, but on food that is natural, healthy, nutritious, and sustainably produced.

By contrast, traditional grocers continue to operate the way they always have: sourcing and selling food and household goods with an emphasis on efficiency and cost savings alone. In 10 to 15 years, when the critical mass of health and environmentally conscious customers becomes a major, highly profitable segment, the market will be dominated by the newer generation of grocery stores and traditional supermarkets that no longer meet changing customer priorities will be wiped out.

How to evaluate changing customer priorities:

1 Go back three to four decades to consider the key customers' priorities that drove their buying decisions. How have these priorities changed over the last few decades?

2 Consider and try to predict emerging trends, behaviors, and forces that will indicate how these priorities will change. You need to make bets on the next generation of customers' decision-making criteria and values, which will influence their buying behavior.

Changing Customer Priorities

Example of changing customer priorities in the food and beverage business over the decades

2000-2020

1. Kids' Nutrition
2. Natural, Authentic
3. Functional Food
4. Environmental Sustainability

1990s

1. Quality
2. Food Nutrition
3. Food Information
4. Pricing

1980s

1. Variety
2. Affordable Choices
3. Packaging

1950s-70s

1. Affordable
2. Accessible

SWOT ANALYSIS

The final step of assessing your position in the environment is to integrate your environmental, resource and capability, and customer priorities analysis. We use the four-quadrant SWOT analysis template to assess the strengths, weaknesses, opportunities, and threats posed by your changing market environment and competitive forces. The analysis is designed to allow innovators to develop strategies to avoid threats, strengthen weaknesses, deepen and broaden strategic capabilities and resources, and capitalize on the emerging market opportunities. The SWOT analysis informs your strategy to reinvent your overarching business design and business model. This strategy determines how you will deliver on your new bets based on your View of the Future.

[*Case in Point*]

SAMPLE SWOT ANALYSIS FOR TOYOTA BEFORE DEVELOPING THE PRIUS

STRENGTHS

- Strong existing brand equity

- Superior and well-developed global distribution

- Cost-efficient and high-quality manufacturing capabilities and centers of competence across the world

- Unique capabilities in new product development and tight supplier-manufacturer network; deep relationships in the auto industry

- Huge domestic Japanese market for early-stage market testing and testing before scaling worldwide

- Cost-efficient use of existing Camry Model chassis auto platform for Prius, which can be used to mount new hybrid engines rather than re-engineering. This allows Toyota to focus on developing the best hybrid engine technology and reliable and efficient manufacturing technology

WEAKNESS

- No precedent in the auto industry

- New capabilities and resources needed

- Nascent market with limited product adoption at early stage

- Underdeveloped supply chain and auto parts infrastructure and innovation ecosystem

- Need for strong supplier-manufacturer collaboration in innovation and new product development

- Huge and risky early-stage capital investment

- Unproven technology; many iterations and corrections required

OPPORTUNITIES

- Signs of global warming

- Growing environmentally conscious consumer base

- Significant cost savings for consumers with fuel-efficient vehicles in light of rising fuel prices

- Governmental legislation that encourages car fuel efficiency

- Slow global economic growth

- OPEC monopoly and limited supply of oil

- Growing car ownership in emerging economies such as the BRICS nations (Brazil, Russia, India, China, South Africa)

THREATS

- Immature and unproven hybrid battery technology leading to car malfunction

- The development of other viable fossil fuel alternatives such as natural gas, biodiesel, and electric cars

- Sudden drop in cost of gas due to increase in supply or disintegration of oil cartels

- Negative impact of Prius sales on Toyota's non-hybrid car sales

- Unknown adverse environmental effects of hybrid manufacturing process

As illustrated by enacting a strategy based on this SWOT, the Prius became a huge win for Toyota:

- Toyota has secured relationships with the best hybrid technology and product suppliers globally.

- The Toyota Prius became the number one selling hybrid vehicle in the world.

- It holds the number one market share for fuel-efficient cars.

- The hybrid technology was extended to Toyota's other vehicles (e.g., Lexus).

ADDRESSING REAL-WORLD TENSIONS THROUGH THE TAO

In Chapter 2 thus far, you have learned about how to anticipate the timing of new market opportunities using analytical tools such as the five forces, resource and capability gaps, changing customer priorities, and the SWOT analysis. The consolidated result of this analysis provides a good indication of the sense of urgency and timing for change that should drive the need to seize new market opportunities. However, the dilemma most enterprises face occurs when the new market opportunity does not precisely match their core competencies.

As you answer this chapter's innovation question, "How do you recognize an opportunity for innovation?," be prepared to face tension between the values of:

| Leveraging existing competencies | VS. | Acquiring new competencies |

Core competencies are a combination of specific skill sets, cumulative knowledge, technical capabilities or business processes, and a business's unique culture. It is an enterprise's distinct competitive advantage, which is normally difficult to replicate. New ventures or start-ups are often still in the process of aggregating their core competencies, but ongoing businesses usually have a well-established set of core competencies that they depend on to create products and services. Because they have already invested a great deal in their existing core competencies, many organization struggle to justify the cost and risk of stepping outside their comfort zone to develop new ones.

When considering areas for new growth, truly innovative market opportunities will usually require new competencies, which can be costly and time consuming to grow internally or acquire externally. At that point, should the company simply walk away from the new opportunity or take it on, using its current set of core competencies, capabilities, and resources?

To reconcile the tension between leveraging existing competencies and acquiring new ones, you need to:

Deepen core competencies to strengthen your competitive advantage and broaden core competencies to address emerging market opportunities.

Acquiring new competencies

Leveraging existing competencies

First, if new market opportunities require diversification that is completely unrelated to your core business, be aware that these attempts at growth are often very risky and unsuccessful. The types of growth and change that are much easier to address are opportunities involving markets or product extensions that are adjacent to or complement your current markets and customers. You can achieve diversification that is related to your core business by growing some internal capabilities (organic growth), combined with external acquisition or strategic alliances to expand an enterprise's portfolio of capabilities and core competencies.

Companies also need to look at their existing internal capabilities and resources to determine whether they are being used to their fullest potential to meet new market opportunities or address unmet needs of existing customers. You can also discover new market opportunities by identifying and resolving structural "pain points" that your existing customers are suffering, which are often due to uncoordinated and fragmented services provided by many unrelated suppliers along the entire industry supply chain network.

[*Case in Point*] CARDINAL HEALTH

In the 1990s, Cardinal Health Inc., a drug distributor that serves in-hospital pharmacies, focused on its core competencies in drug sorting and delivery. Over time, the company identified their customers' key pain points and unmet needs. Hospital pharmacies faced critical challenges such as high staff turnover, a shortage of pharmacists, drug contamination, or incorrect drug prescriptions which combined to make the pharmacies unprofitable. Cardinal Health had to decide whether to continue focusing on its existing core competencies or to invest in acquiring new competencies to meet the challenges it had identified.

Cardinal Health created a strategy to build on its existing competencies of drug quality and delivery while expanding into automatic drug dispensing by acquiring Pyxis Corporation. The Pyxis MedStation system was developed as an automatic drug dispensing machine (like an ATM for banks) to reduce the risk of dangerous drug interactions and incorrect prescriptions, and to benefit from improved automatic billing systems and inventory control. The acquisition allowed the company to expand exponentially into the broader business of managing and operating pharmacies on behalf of hospitals, turning a once ailing operation under the hospitals' management into a profitable one, using their existing and newly acquired technologies and systems. In the early 2000s, they continued to expand into a new area of their business, moving beyond pharmacies to supply surgical products, tools, and equipment to surgical rooms in the hospitals they served. Today, Cardinal Health is a huge company with more than $101 billion in sales and $23 billion in market capitalization compared to its 1999 revenue of approximately $10 billion.

How do you recognize an opportunity for innovation?

Answering this question starts with the practice of:

Scanning Your Environment

▼ Conduct Porter's five forces and PEST environmental analyses to identify the key changing forces that can fundamentally alter the dynamics of your industry and future competition.

▼ Conduct an internal analysis to determine how urgently your organization needs to change and whether you need to develop or acquire new resources and capabilities to meet the expected changes in your industry and to align with your new bets.

▼ Draw a changing customers' priority strategy map to chart the history of customer purchasing priorities and how you predict it will change in the next 5 to 10 years.

▼ Assess the effectiveness of the current strategy in view of the dynamic changes by doing a SWOT analysis.

Want to go deeper?

Further Reading

Porter, M. (1980). *Competitive strategy*. New York, NY: Free Press.

Porter, M. (1985). *Competitive advantage*. New York, NY: Free Press.

Porter, M. (1998). *On competition*. Boston, MA: Harvard Business School Publishing Corp.

Chandler, A. (1962). *Strategy and structure: Chapters in the history of the industrial enterprise*. Cambridge, MA: Massachusetts Institute of Technology Press

Prahalad, C. K. and Hamel, G. (1990). *The core competence of the corporation*. Boston, MA: Harvard Business School Publishing Corp.

CHAPTER 3 | MARSH 泽

How do you compete to outsmart established players?

Marsh symbolizes "the way"
to answer this question.

Marsh FILTERS. Marshes are rich
with nutrients and wildlife, yet
murky and full of danger. This
element teaches us to avoid
waters where you might drown
and seek clear waters where you
can thrive.

Marsh represents the practice
of Crafting a Smart Innovation
Strategy.

How do you compete to outsmart established players?

WHY IS THIS QUESTION IMPORTANT?

More than 90% of new product ideas fail. And more than 80% of new businesses fail within their first year. Success doesn't occur by chance, hard work, or even the greatness of the idea. If you take a step back and study innovations that have managed to beat the odds, you can learn from the characteristics of strategies that increase your likelihood of gaining traction and succeeding in the market.

*W*hile entrepreneurs and innovators passionately believe in the potential of their ideas, not all innovations are created equal. The majority of innovations tend to be incremental in nature. Incremental innovation consists mostly of tweaking product performance or processes, which may have varying degrees of impact on an industry (e.g., a razor with five blades compared to the previous model with four); these are not game-changing innovations. If you are a new player in a market or a relatively small firm, you are constantly competing against incumbent competitors that are richer, bigger, faster, and stronger, so to speak. Even the giants in an industry compete with others' evolutions of existing offerings, and are often eclipsed by a rival's newest iteration of product performance. So how do you compete and win against the incumbents?

This chapter's focus is on how to devise a strategy that will help you overcome the disadvantages of being a new player or introducing a new product or service amid existing players. Your innovation strategy needs to ensure that you avoid competing head on with big players, entering markets that are too crowded, and releasing ideas that are too incremental. Rather than entering a deadly game that you can't win, reinvent the game, make new rules and become the new leader. Innovations that have succeeded in beating out industry giants and revolutionizing an industry incorporate a few important innovation strategies.

This chapter presents five major innovation strategies that I have found to be the most applicable to the existing innovation landscape. One or more may be more relevant to your organization, product, or service than another. They provide lessons that might be applicable to your innovation or industry. While this is not an exhaustive list of innovation strategies, successful ones tend to fall into these five. Your innovation strategy is key to increasing chances for success, especially in an 80/20 Ð 20/80 game-changing shift.

STEPS FOR YOUR ACTION PLAN	WHAT THEY HELP YOU ACCOMPLISH
Consider applying blue ocean strategy innovation	Gain advantage over incumbents who compete in the same market with somewhat similar competitive elements by eliminating some elements and adding new, innovative ones to create uncontested new market space
Consider applying demand innovation	Gain advantage in mature industries that seem to have reached a plateau by creating new value upstream or downstream of your value chain
Consider applying disruptive innovation	Gain advantage in a market in which there is evidence of overserving customer needs by introducing simpler products
Consider applying big bang disruption innovation	Gain advantage over multiple industries by creating cheaper and better, customized, and integrated products, using technology to displace incumbents
Consider applying dilemma reconciliation innovation	Gain advantage through synthesizing seemingly contradictory values or elements to solve hidden tensions to create lasting competitive advantage

BLUE OCEAN STRATEGY

Created by W. Chan Kim and Renée Mauborgne, co-directors of the Blue Ocean Strategy Institute at INSEAD, *Blue Ocean Strategy* is a bestselling book across five continents, having won numerous awards for the strategy's importance and impact in the field of business management. *Blue Ocean Strategy* states that the business market is divided into two oceans: a red and a blue one.

The red ocean is the existing, crowded market space in which organizations compete head-to-head in a bloody red ocean of rivals fighting over market share, demand, and a shrinking profit pool. Business strategy hinges on either offering a similar product at a lower cost or creating a differentiated product and charging a premium for it. Regardless of whether you choose to compete in the low, middle, or high end of the market, there will eventually be enough competitors to erode profits and mimic what their competitors do to at least some extent. As more companies chase the same market, it gets more crowded and profits and growth are reduced.

On the other hand, blue oceans are new, undefined markets without competition; they are untouched, vast, and deep, which invites profitable growth. Demand is created rather than fought over. Competition is irrelevant because the rules of the market have not yet been created. Business strategy centers on creating uncontested market space that is ripe for growth. In short, red ocean strategy is about market competition, whereas blue ocean strategy is about market creation.

The way to create a new market in the industry is to ask four key questions:

ELIMINATE
Which factors should be eliminated that the industry takes for granted and assumes that all customers want?

CREATE
Which factors should be created that the industry has never offered?

REDUCE
Which factors should be reduced well below industry standard?

RAISE
Which factors should be raised well above industry standard?

Curves is a well-cited example of blue ocean strategy. Curves, also known as Curves for Women, Curves Fitness, or Curves International, is a women-only gym franchise. In 2004, it was worth an estimated $2.6 billion. During its inception its founders recognized that the gym and fitness franchise market was a saturated red ocean. Basic health clubs were competing with trendy facilities in urban settings, with specialized equipment, fancy locker rooms, saunas, and juice bars. The client experience was designed around workout times of one hour or longer. Membership fees could be $100 or more per month.

Curves created a blue ocean of demand for a new health club experience. It focused entirely on women, primarily in the suburbs, who do not have a lot of time to work out. They opened locations in the suburbs, with ample parking. They got rid of expensive machines, with only about 10 machines arranged in a semi-circle to facilitate interaction between members. It takes 30 minutes to use all of the equipment in the series, which consist of hydraulic exercise machines that are easy to use and do not require adjusting. A women-only gym creates a less judgmental atmosphere, which many women find more comfortable than a typical health club environment. Overheads are low; there are no fancy changing-rooms, just a curtain, and there are no showers or other amenities. This keeps membership costs low, averaging $30 a month. Curves facilities are located in most towns in America.

In summary, this is how Curves created a blue ocean strategy:

ELIMINATE: Men, TV monitors and screens/frills, downtown locations

CREATE: Social safe place to work out, all-women gym, free parking

REDUCE: Membership costs, expensive complicated equipment, time to complete a workout (short 30 minutes)

RAISE: Convenience/proximity to suburbs

What Can You Learn from Blue Ocean Strategy?

Rather than being another player in an overcrowded market, create new market space that is uncontested by competition and ripe for growth.

The Strategy Canvas of Curves

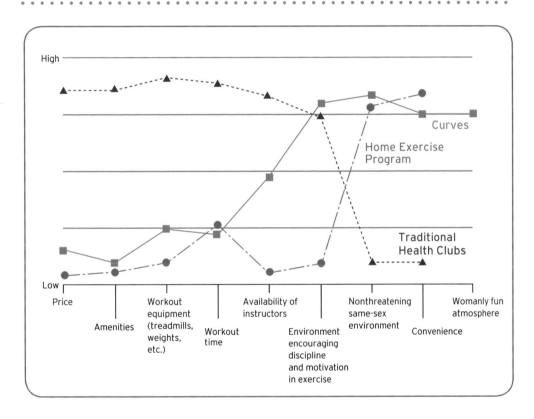

"There comes a point at which improving upon the thing that was important in the past is a bad move... It's actually feeding competitive advantage to outsiders by not recognizing the value of other qualities."
—Clay Shirkey, professor of new media studies, New York University

Want to go deeper?

Further Reading

Kim, W. C. and Mauborgne, R. (2005). *Blue ocean strategy: How to create uncontested market space and make the competition irrelevant*. Boston, MA: Harvard Business School Press.

DEMAND INNOVATION

The concept of demand innovation was invented by strategy consultant Adrian Slywotzky and is explained in his book, *How to Grow When Markets Don't*, co-authored by Richard Wise and Karl Weber. Slywotzky is a partner at Oliver Wyman, a leading global management consulting firm, and is an influential thought-leader on business management. Slywotzky contends that you don't always have to invent a new product to grow your market. In fact, in most industries it is increasingly difficult to develop a new product that is truly different from all others. Completely new products often require development of a new customer base, in a different market, and acquisition of new distribution channels, challenging variables which often lead to a very high failure rate. Demand innovation is about shifting away from the notion of developing a breakthrough product to focusing on discovering new customer demands that exist upstream or downstream from your existing offering.

When pursuing demand innovation, you must examine your company's resources and capabilities to see whether they are underutilized and can be further exploited to help your customers solve significant pain points and bottlenecks embedded in your industry value chain. You want to identify in your value chain (upstream, midstream, or downstream) where you can offer high value service solutions for your existing customer base.

In his book, Slywotzky uses John Deere Landscapes to explain demand innovation. Deere and Company was founded in 1837 by Illinois blacksmith John Deere. It is a leading farm equipment company, producing plows, cultivators, tractors, and equipment for use in construction, forestry, and lawn care. Its business is very much dependent on the cyclical economics of agriculture and crop harvesting which are very susceptible to weather conditions. To improve its performance, cost cutting alone could not deliver the return on investment its shareholders expected. Growth is an important element of the company's continued success.

In 2001, John Deere looked at its Commercial and Consumer Equipment Division, which makes lawn mowing, landscaping, and turf care equipment and serves the green landscaping industry with sales of about $2.5 billion, a quarter of total company sales. At that time, the industry was growing 10% to 15% faster than the agriculture farm equipment industry with an annual volume of about $110 billion. A close examination of the landscaping industry revealed a great opportunity for the company to address the badly served, fragmented landscaping industry with many small-sized local and regional distributors. To complete a job, landscapers had to supply the lawn maintenance supplies (buying them from John Deere), but also the trees, shrubs, sprinkler systems, irrigation systems, plants, planting materials, fertilizers, mulch, plant foods and pesticides, rocks, and road pavement. By following these customers closely to see what happened to the tractors after they bought from John Deere, they found that their customers would typically require many different contractors to complete the job, which caused many complex coordination challenges and complexities. Landscapers spent a lot of time and effort trying to coordinate these activities amid a fragmented supply chain to complete a landscaping project (e.g., community parks, golf courses, and school yards) on time.

In 2000, John Deere established a new division called John Deere Landscapes and the following year began to acquire two leading distributor chains: McGinnis Farms, a landscaping materials (trees, shrubs, and landscaping gear) wholesaler in Atlanta, and Richton International, an irrigation system equipment and outdoor lighting distributor in Michigan. John Deere integrated these two companies' activities to help solve their customers' pain points in attempting to provide seamless one-stop shop convenience. It also offered online credit approval financing services through its John Deere Credit operations to contractors who needed cash flow to fund larger landscaping projects.

Today, John Deere Landscapes is the most profitable business in the John Deere Corporation, with more than 400 branches in the United States and Canada. The company focuses on serving landscape, irrigation, and turf care professionals. It carries product lines in lawn care supplies, nursery stock, irrigation, and landscape supplies and lighting. The company used its strong relationship with existing customers to offer them new product lines, leveraged its existing resources and capabilities to meet their larger, unmet needs, and eliminated bottlenecks caused by a highly fragmented industry. This type of business model, driven by demand innovation, is both low risk and high growth.

What Can You Learn from Demand Innovation?

- Introducing new products is a difficult way to achieve market growth in a mature industry.

- Innovation and growth opportunities can be found by offering higher-value service solutions that are linked to product experience, especially in industries with fragmented value chains and poorly integrated services; this opportunity carries lower risk because it is difficult for your competitors to copy.

Want to go deeper?

Further Reading

Slywotzky, A., Wise, R. and Weber, K. (2003). *Demand innovation: How to grow when markets don't*. New York, NY: Warner Books.

Slywotzky, A. (2011). *Demand: Creating what people love before they know they want it*. New York, NY: Crown Business.

DISRUPTIVE INNOVATION

Disruptive innovation is a term coined by Clayton Christensen, a Harvard Business School professor, and was first discussed in the book *The Innovator's Dilemma* (1997), which won the Global Business Book Award for the best business book of the year. Christensen is widely regarded as one of the world's foremost experts on innovation and growth. Disruptive innovation is a business theory that describes how a new innovation can disrupt an existing market and eventually trigger the growth of an entirely new one. In his book, Christensen proposes two types of innovation: sustaining and disruptive. Sustaining innovations are based on incremental change. They perpetuate the current business model. Over time, a sustaining innovation strategy will likely lead you to develop features that overserve or exceed most consumers' needs. For example, who needs a razor blade with five blades when you already have one with four?

As an overview, disruptive innovations are based on producing simple, "good enough" products that are often not technologically sophisticated at a low cost that appeal to consumers with few and basic needs—the bottom of the market or a market which did not exist yet because the incumbent product was too expensive or too complex to use. The "disruption" begins when the innovation captures the bottom of the market, then rapidly improves its features and functionality and begins to take more and more customers from the incumbent(s) and eventually displaces established players. Successful disruptive innovation strategy can transform an industry in a game-changing way. It enables people to do more complex and sophisticated tasks in a less expensive and more convenient setting that are normally done by highly trained specialists in a more sophisticated environment. A good example of disruptive innovation in the health care industry is nurse practitioners in walk-in, neighborhood-clinics or drug stores who perform simple rule-based medical diagnoses and treatment and thus replace the need for patients to seek such routine services from a physician in a general hospital.

The Disruptive Innovation Model

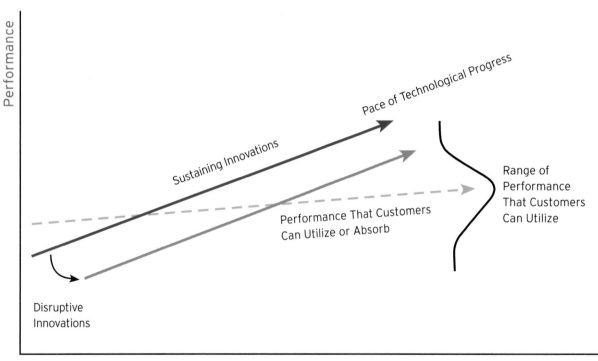

Source: From *The Innovator's Solution* by Clayton Christensen and Michael Raynor, copyright ©2003. Used with permission of Harvard Business Publishing Corporation.

This figure explains disruptive innovation in more depth. In disruptive innovation circumstances, the incumbents produce a product that is useful and good enough to customers. The average needs of customers for such products increase slowly over time (orange line) and there is a distribution range of needs across the customer base illustrated by the bell curve on the far right—some have more needs and some have fewer. The incumbent continues to incrementally improve the product over time (sustaining innovation) (blue line); but the pace of technological and product improvement soon outpaces the average consumer's needs (blue line crosses above the orange line). Thus, continued product refinement overserves the average consumer's needs. For example, newer models of microwaves or washing machines have many functions and codes that the average consumer does not use or need. In sustaining innovation, the big giant leaders always win—they are already established, and have larger research and development departments, better distribution channels, more brand recognition, etc. Low-end disruptive innovation occurs when a new competitor creates a much simpler version of the product, which is often technologically simpler and good enough to appeal to the consumers with the fewest and most modest needs (green line). The target customer of the disruptive innovation does not need the full performance valued by the high-need end of the market; the target customer is happy with a "good-enough" and economical product. The incumbent leaders don't compete fiercely in this market because it serves consumers who are unwilling to pay a premium for the enhancements in product performance. But over time, the disruptive innovation also improves its functionality and slowly begins to gain more and more market share. As it improves, the product still has lower performance than the incumbent, but now begins to exceed the requirements of more of the market with low but not the lowest needs. Eventually, the disruptive innovation continues to improve its "good-enough" product to meet the needs of the average consumer and win over the most profitable segment of the market (green line crosses above the orange line). In this way, it can overtake and replace the incumbent. But it too can ultimately overserve the average consumer and be susceptible to a new disruptive innovation.

Dr. Christensen has used the historic case of steamboats vs. sailboats in his teachings to illustrate disruptive innovation. In the late 1800s, sailing clipper ships were the main mode of transporting goods between continents, having been perfected over hundreds of years of incremental change. Examples of sailboat design that improved incrementally over time include different hull shapes to increase tonnage and an additional mast to increase speed; these are examples of sustaining innovation. In contrast, the steamboat represents disruptive innovation. Initially, the steam engine was very inefficient, and as a result, the steamboat only competed with the sailboat for inland water routes. Sailboat shipping lines viewed inland water routes as less profitable compared to the profit margin on seagoing routes anyway. However, steamboats had a different way of doing business. They did not depend on uncontrollable wind patterns and could stay on schedule. Over time, the steam engine became more efficient and improved to the point where it could compete and eventually overtake the cost advantage of sailboats. In addition, new transportation routes opened that were difficult for sailing ships to use (e.g., the Suez Canal that opened a shortcut between Asia and Europe in 1869); this caused the steam engine to began to overtake the sailboat's market share. Eventually, the steamboat replaced the sailboat as the main transport vehicle and transformed the industry of moving goods across waters.

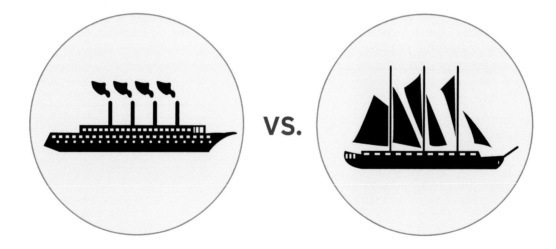

VS.

In 1983, Sony released the first camcorder meant for non-professional consumer use called the Betamovie BMC-100P. Over the next two decades the consumer camcorder market grew quickly, evolving through different storage formats and recording technologies that provided users with longer recording time, better picture quality, and reduced size and weight. With the advent of digital technology, camcorders became "tapeless" but still required the use of memory cards.

Then along came the Flip. The Flip Video camera was a series of pocket-sized, tapeless, and user-friendly camcorders introduced by Pure Digital Technologies in 2006. The entrepreneurs behind Flip initially experimented with low-cost, single-use digital cameras sold in drugstores but soon realized the shortcomings of their business model, which required users to promptly return their cameras to stores in order to get their prints developed and a CD. However the key lesson learned, which led to the birth of the Flip Video, was that customers were willing to sacrifice image quality for access to a cheap and easier-to-use device. They saw an opportunity to bring the simplicity of point-and-shoot cameras to videography.

Small enough to fit into your pocket, the Flip Video only offered the most basic functions of record, zoom, playback, and browse buttons. The manufacturer had consciously eliminated the complexity of digital camcorders, which had features such as image stabilization, night vision mode, and color correction but were not desired by the average user (as another example of overserving the customer's needs). Another key innovation was a built-in USB port to allow hassle-free uploading of video clips—literally delivering on the promise of "plug and play," and lowering the barrier of the post-production editing process. At an affordable price range of about $200 (especially in comparison to that of digital camcorders), they were an instant hit and began to seriously threaten the camcorder market. The company subsequently released smaller models with high definition recording, longer recording time, and larger viewing screens.

In 2009, tech giant Cisco acquired Flip for $590 million. By then, Flip had sold 2 million units and many speculated the move was motivated by Cisco's desire to expand its presence in the consumer electronics market. Unfortunately, in 2011, Cisco decided to shut down the Flip division. It is rumored that the main factor in this decision was the emerging use of smartphones to capture video. The Flip, which had once disrupted the camcorder industry, was then itself disrupted by the smartphone industry.

In short, at the peak of Flip's success, the manufacturer managed to disrupt the camcorder industry and create a new consumer video market because, while existing camcorder companies focused on traditional advancements such as fidelity, resolution, and technical features, Flip recognized the unmet user needs of convenience, simplicity, affordability, and shareability. However, without considering the emerging advancement of smartphone technology which incorporated video, it became a victim of newer disruptive technology as well.

What Can You Learn from Disruptive Innovation?

- As a new player, your offering cannot just be incrementally better than those of established players. It must address a significant pain point or need that the existing market is failing to meet.

- When an industry begins to overserve mass consumer needs, this is a sign that it is ripe for disruptive innovation.

- Initially, keep your offering focused on serving a simple need at a lower cost. As adoption grows, technology advances, and you reach a critical mass of customers who understand your value, you can broaden your offering.

Want to go deeper?

Further Reading

Christensen, C. (1997). *The innovator's dilemma*. Boston, MA: Harvard Business School Press.

Christensen, C. and Raynor, M. (2003). *The innovator's solution*. Boston, MA: Harvard Business School Press.

BIG BANG DISRUPTION INNOVATION

Big bang disruption is a term created by Larry Downes and Paul F. Nunes, a research fellow and Global Managing Director of Research respectively, at the Accenture Institute for High Performance. In their book, *Big Bang Disruption* (2014), they explain that more than ever before, today's innovations (especially Internet-based applications or products) have the potential to replace existing business models and established incumbents in a flash. Rather than entering a market as a product or service that is either inferior and cheaper or more expensive and superior than competing offerings (as is the case with Disruptive Innovation), a big bang disruption occurs when a newly introduced product or service is both better and cheaper from the moment of creation and immediately becomes a widely sought after commodity. There are three features of big bang disruptive innovation that defy conventional wisdom:

Conventional wisdom focuses on a low-cost or premium product or customer relationship. But big bang innovations focus on all three dimensions at once: the products/services are better, cheaper, and customized at the outset.

Conventional wisdom focuses on finding a small group of early adopters for the new commodity and later introducing it into the mainstream market. But big bang innovations market to all customer segments immediately—with a winner-take-all result if the launch is successful. This type of innovation does not have carefully timed marketing campaigns or separate product releases to different customer groups.

Conventional wisdom focuses on experimentation particularly in lower-cost, feature-poor technologies that meet the needs of underserved customer segments. Big bang innovators launch low-cost, often random experiments of combinations of off-the-shelf parts, software, and loosely connected service providers. They launch without a business model or business plan directly in the market with real users serving as collaborators. Most will fail. But it only takes one from a competitor to succeed to devastate the business model.

Big bang disruption is fueled by new technologies, such as broadband networks, cloud-based computing, and increasingly powerful mobile devices, because they drastically reduce the cost of information, product creation, and experimentation. Moreover, while in the past, technological advances resulted in products with short life spans for digital businesses, which were a relatively small segment of the business world, today *every* business has a digital component.

Traditionally, one would apply the Everett Rogers diffusion of innovation curve for market adoption, which is a bell curve outlining five distinct market segments starting with innovators (2.5%), followed by early adopters (13.5%), early majority (34%), late majority (34%), and laggards (16%). However, big bang disruption is characterized by relatively short blasts of market penetration and market saturation. Therefore, big bang disruption has only two phases—trial users followed by everybody else—and more resembles a narrow shark's fin instead of a bell curve. And this transition from a small to a large group of users occurs very quickly: in a matter of months, sometimes even weeks. Market penetration often occurs nearly instantaneously (hence the "Big Bang"). For software-based products, innovators may sign up millions of users in a matter of days. Then, as the disruptor quickly approaches saturation, adoption drops at nearly the same pace at which it took off, leading to a period of rapid decline.

Big Bang Market Adoption

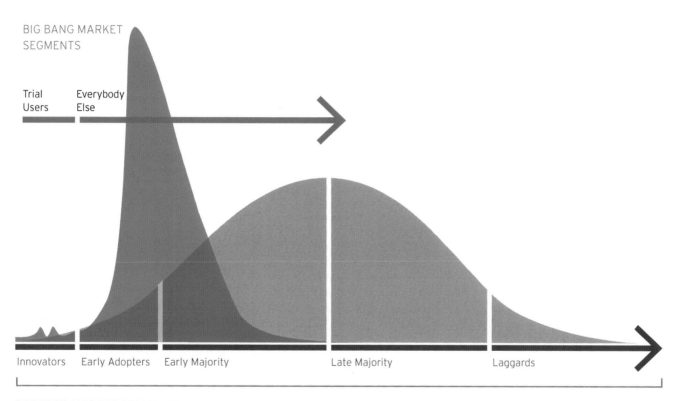

BIG BANG MARKET
SEGMENTS

Trial
Users

Everybody
Else

Innovators Early Adopters Early Majority   Late Majority   Laggards

ROGERS'S MARKET SEGMENTS

Source: From *Big Bang Disruption: Strategy in the Age of Devastating Innovation* by Larry Downes and Paul
Nunes, copyright © 2014. Used by permission of Portfolio, an imprint of Penguin Group (USA) LLC.

A good example is the GPS portable navigation device for cars. Up until a few years ago, drivers happily paid more than a few hundred dollars for a portable GPS device that could be mounted on the car's dashboard. But as smartphones exploded in popularity, free navigation apps became available allowing for hand-held GPS capability. These phone apps, such as Google Maps, were also more accurate and performed better than portable GPS devices. Eighteen months after the debut of navigation tools for phones, leading GPS device manufacturers had lost 85% of their market value.

What Can You Learn from Big Bang Disruption?

- Watch out for experimental product launches from start-ups that possess big bang disruption features. It can destroy your business, even if it's a mature one, in a hurry.

- Leverage the Internet, computing, and digital and broadband technology to take advantage of low-cost and quick innovation to develop new iterations and fine-tune your business model hypotheses. This is the best time to innovate with the right technology and business model mix to come up with faster, cheaper, better, and more customized and integrated products right from the start to displace competitors' goods or services.

- Your user is your R&D partner, your best salesman, and your reference customers. Leverage your user community and social media to create big bang disruption.

Want to go deeper?

Further Reading

Downes, L. and Nunes, P. (2014). *Big bang disruption: Strategy in the age of devastating innovation.* New York, NY: Penguin Group.

DILEMMA RECONCILIATION INNOVATION

Charles Hampden-Turner, my PhD supervisor at Cambridge University, is a Cambridge and Harvard trained British management philosopher, and senior research associate at the Cambridge Judge Business School, Cambridge University. He pioneered the concept of creating wealth through reconciling paradoxes and dilemmas in his book *Building Cross-Cultural Competencies*. When people hear the word innovation, they often think of new, ingenious inventions but innovation need not be completely original; it often involves old elements in new combinations. Dilemma reconciliation innovation is about combining elements that are seemingly unrelated to each other or that even conflict to form a new product or service or improve an existing one.

One of the greatest and most simple examples of dilemma reconciliation is the traffic light. Decoupled, the red light signals stop and the green signals go, which are opposing values. The concept of the traffic light is an amazing innovation because it managed to combine two seemingly conflicting ideas into one system. Red and green are a continuous loop with yellow serving as a critical transition signal. The result of this reconciliation is that we have a universal way of managing traffic safely.

The yin-yang is a quintessential example of dilemma reconciliation. The yin-yang is used as an important and recurring metaphor in the Tao of Innovation to help resolve real-world tensions to overcome organizational resistance to change.

Toyota entered the luxury car market using dilemma reconciliation with its Lexus model. To compete with its rivals, Mercedes, BMW, and Cadillac, rather than choosing a single dimension to differentiate its car, Toyota combined low cost (value) and differentiation (luxury) strategies. It used the low-cost Toyota Camry chassis, which was produced in the millions, as the platform for all Lexus models and mounted sophisticated features on the dashboard. Lexus used this dual strategy to produce a luxury car that costs less to produce and buy than those made by other leading automobile producers and to introduce the Lexus in an already crowded luxury car market within a relatively short period of time. It has successfully built a quality premium brand with a loyal following of discerning luxury consumers.

What Can You Learn from Dilemma Reconciliation?

- Innovation that resolves pain points with a single dimensional approach is easy to copy, whereas innovation that synthesizes values or elements in tension with one another creates lasting competitive advantage and sustainability. Opportunities lie where there are tensions, paradoxes, or dilemmas between conflicting values that you are trying to reconcile.

Want to go deeper?

Further Reading

Hampden-Turner, C. and Trompenaars, F. (2000). *Building cross-cultural competencies: How to create wealth from conflicting values*. New Haven, CT: Yale University Press.

Hampden-Turner, C. and Trompenaars, F. (2010). *Riding the waves of innovation: Harness the power of global culture to drive creativity and growth*. New York, NY: McGraw-Hill.

This chapter describes how to grow and innovate using different types of innovation strategies. Innovation can be demand innovation, blue ocean, sustaining or disruptive innovation, or big bang disruption, or often a combination of some or all of the above elements of successful strategies. Some types of innovation strategies involve high risk; but others can dramatically lower the risk of innovation if done correctly. Risk is one of the more difficult aspects to embrace when innovating, particularly for more established firms, which tend to be much more risk averse than start-ups and entrepreneurs. Regardless of which innovation models you choose to mitigate risk and maximize rewards, one common dilemma is the choice between sustaining growth in existing markets or disrupting your current business to address new market opportunities that extend beyond your current resources and capabilities.

As you answer this chapter's innovation question, "How do you compete to outsmart established players?," be prepared to face tension between the values of:

SUSTAINING VS. **DISRUPTING**

Sustaining innovation is usually based on responding to incremental changes in customer needs. It may result in a faster, better, or cheaper version of an existing offering. Although this is not easy to accomplish, it is the safer path that allows you to continue your current practices and leverage your existing resources and capabilities.

Disruptive innovation is a creative type of destruction that can replace your existing business over time, beginning with products that meet the needs of future consumers or existing customers who have basic (low-end rather than high-end) needs and expectations. Disruptions are mostly carried out by new players outside the industry or start-ups that have no vested interest in the current value-creating process.

Disrupting

Sustaining

To reconcile the tension between sustaining, incremental innovation and disruptive, game-changing innovation, you need to:

Disrupt your business with lower-risk innovation before it can be disrupted by the new players or competition.

To minimize risk over time, existing firms need to pursue opportunities to disrupt themselves by producing lower-cost and more basic products while continuing to meet current customer needs by generating new and improved offerings and pursuing sustaining innovation. Self-disruption should be pursued outside the existing organization using a different risk-reward yardstick to nurture disruptive product ideas or through mergers and acquisitions to invest in start-up ventures with disruptive innovation potential.

In this day and age, the ultimate product and services should be designed to:

- create new value and customer benefits;

- utilize modular product concepts, allowing one-to-one personalized customization;

- leverage social media for business and customer benefit, including user community feedback loops for improving products and services;

- be integrated and inter-operable with other related products;

- significantly simplify processes and the system's total cost rather than upfront product cost reduction alone.

Innovation that is not able to deliver some of the key benefits mentioned above is too incremental to make a real positive impact. Durable innovation creates values that combine seemingly contradictory elements to help resolve customers' key tensions and pain points that competitors and the market have failed to detect or ignored.

DELL COMPUTERS

Dell started in the early 1980s with Michael Dell's $1,000 investment, when he was a college student, into reconfiguring and customizing old tabletop computers for fellow student customers. The company is well known for its supply chain management, particularly its direct-sales model and its "built to order" approach. Dell pioneered the concept of mass customization and leveraging the Internet for built-to-order direct sales. The concept of synthesizing low-cost, high-speed mass production with modular customization features drove PC production costs down dramatically, thus allowing more consumers to afford participation in the digital revolution. Using this model, Dell became the number one personal computer producer in the world in the 1990s.

However, in the 2000s, Dell, like other personal computer producers, has suffered as consumers switch from desktops and laptops to tablet computing (e.g., Apple's iPad). Moreover, its mobility division has not succeeded in developing smartphones or tablets. Meanwhile, other competitors such as Lenovo, Asus, and Acer have lowered production costs and increased competition in the non-premium sector. This has caused Dell to slip to the third position globally and second largest in the world with roughly $60 billion in sales revenue and a net income of $2.5 billion.

In 2013, Michael Dell reacted to this decline and increasing threat to his business by taking important steps to disrupt and reinvent his company. First, he executed a painful $24 billion buy-out deal to return his company to a privately held rather than a publicly listed status to avoid the pressures of having to play Wall Street's short-term quarterly earning games and have the freedom to "self-disrupt." This freed Dell to focus on the development and application of thin client networks and cloud computing in which connected network systems share computing needs and capacities to save on the total cost of ownership and dramatically improve efficiency. Finally, in alignment with its new technology focus, Dell acquired Wyse ($500 million), a maker of PCs with all data accessed via a USB port that is connected to the cloud, to leverage Wyse's advances in cloud computing technology. Dell is setting itself up for a creative self-disruption and a potential turnaround before it is totally disrupted by competition and other substitutable products and services.

How do you compete to outsmart established players?

Answering this question starts with the practice of:

Crafting a Smart Innovation Strategy

Determine whether the following innovation strategy or strategies can apply to your industry and innovation idea:

▼ If disruptive innovation is applicable to you, identify how your innovation is a simpler, cheaper, and/or less technologically sophisticated product that will appeal to customers with more basic needs and expectations. Assess whether you can improve features and functionality rapidly to capture more market share and eventually displace established competitors.

▼ If blue ocean strategy is applicable to you, identify the factors in your industry to eliminate, create, reduce, and raise.

▼ If demand innovation is applicable to you, create a value chain map that identifies pain points in the upstream, midstream, and downstream of the entire industry value chain. Develop ideas to significantly simplify complex processes, resolve key pain points and discontinuities, and explore opportunities for co-creation, one-to-one marketing, or mass customization.

▼ If big bang disruption is applicable to you, identify how to leverage technology to help you create a better, cheaper, and more customized product or service.

▼ If dilemma reconciliation is applicable to you, identify the key tensions or trade-offs when customers use the current product. Develop a dilemma reconciliation that synthesizes the two sets of values that are in tension into a virtuous concept of duality that embraces both trade-offs.

The following table helps you to evaluate the opportunities for introducing a combination of innovative strategies in your business model. In principle, the more innovative elements your ideation and business model have the better it is.

YOUR INNOVATION	BLUE OCEAN INNOVATION	DEMAND INNOVATION	DISRUPTIVE INNOVATION	BIG BANG DISRUPTION INNOVATION	DILEMMA RECONCILIATION INNOVATION
Product/Service Innovation	Yes/No	Yes/No	Yes/No	Yes/No	Yes/No
Business model Innovation	Yes/No	Yes/No	Yes/No	Yes/No	Yes/No

How do you move beyond the status quo?

WIND 风

FIRE 火

THUNDER 雷

YIN-YANG 阴阳

EARTH 坤

MOUNTAIN 艮

MARSH 泽

WATER 水

HEAVEN 天

Heaven symbolizes
to answer this question.

Heaven TRANSCENDS. It is an
aspirational space, unencumbered
by the constraints of the ever
world. This element teach
to envision new paradig
experiences that t
higher plane.

Heave
In

How do you move beyond the status quo?

WHY IS THIS QUESTION IMPORTANT?

Most organizations aspire to be innovative and think outside the box, yet when it comes to developing ideas and solutions, many resist deviating from their standard operating procedures and any challenges to the status quo. So where do innovative blue ocean ideas come from, especially if you don't have a revolutionary genius like Steve Jobs or deep pockets to hire award-winning consultants? How do you enable creative thinking and experimentation that can lead to promising market opportunities and breakthrough ideas?

"We can't solve problems by using the same kind of thinking we used when we created them." –Albert Einstein

*I*n this chapter, I highlight a handful of key ideation practices rooted in the world of design thinking. Design thinking can be traced back to fields such as industrial design, engineering, and architecture, which involve understandting end users' needs and behaviors and allowing them to directly inform and inspire the creative process of design, conceptualization, and the crafting of meaningful solutions. Design is often thought to be specific to developing tangible objects, such as more ergonomic furniture or attractive objects. However, over the years, design and innovation firms, such as IDEO, have brought human-centered design thinking to the attention of business and systems thinkers who are looking for new ways of tackling complex problems. More and more innovators realize that the same methodologies used to design products can be applied to intangible challenges as diverse as redefining brand experiences, inventing new services, rethinking public systems, and solving social crises. Today, design thinking has become recognized as an intuitive, creative, and generative approach to concept development and problem solving, often offering a refreshing alternative to more linear, analytical, or scientific approaches.

STEPS FOR YOUR ACTION PLAN

Find inspiration through user empathy

Seek out analogous inspiration

Solve problems with interdisciplinary teams

Learn through prototyping and experimentation

WHAT THEY HELP YOU ACCOMPLISH

Discover untapped opportunities through your customers' significant pain points by getting up close and personal

Gain inspiration from understanding how other industries outside your competitive landscape solved similar problems

Problem solve creatively by working with diverse disciplines and perspectives

Gain feedback quickly through rough experimentation and fast cycles of iteration

FIND INSPIRATION THROUGH USER EMPATHY

People lie at the heart of almost every business or organizational chal-lenge. While this seems obvious, the reality is that many innovations are conceived and developed without a deep understanding of the people they are meant to serve. In the age of information, we have more facts and figures than ever before, but suffer a dire lack of empathy for what people actually need, want, and value. Unearthing customer pain points (which are aspects of a product, service, or experience that cause frustration, wast-ing of time and resources, or even actual harm) is the richest source of clues for where new opportunities lie. When we take the time to personally understand who we are designing offerings for, we make better creative and business decisions to follow.

When applying design thinking, the ideation process begins when we seek opportunities to address customers' unmet needs and pain points. Developing and exercising empathy can be an intuitive and easy way to gain insights. The best way to do this is to "walk a mile in someone else's shoes."

For example:

- Rather than trying to create more patient-centered health care through collecting surveys, sit down with a patient to understand what they went through in fighting a disease or tag along on a hospital visit.

- Rather than holding a brainstorming session to come up with assumptions about what kind of toothbrush people will want in the future, spend an hour observing how different people go through their entire morning or night-time oral care routines.

- Rather than guessing what teenagers think is cool, go to the mall to observe groups of friends shopping or at home online in their natural environment.

In short, put yourself in the customer's shoes and walk through the customer experience firsthand.

Distinct from quantitative or survey-based research methods, empathy or learning firsthand about the feelings, thoughts, or attitudes of another person or group is less about gaining proof or validation and more about acquiring inspiration and qualitative insights. Empathic exercises get you out of your own reality (which can be limiting and lead to faulty assumptions) and into the minds and worlds of the people you are designing solutions for. When done upstream in the innovation process, these personal experiences can uncover opportunities that would otherwise remain obscured by facts and figures or your own preconceived notions.

It's about discovering opportunities through user empathy and identifying pain points.

USER EMPATHY: WHERE TO START...

→ Be a fly on the wall and observe the behaviors of people in their natural environments, which might include how they navigate through processes, their consumption habits, social and emotional interactions between people, and how people react to objects or communicate.

→ Walk through the process or encounter that you are designing for from the perspective of a user or customer (undercover if necessary to be treated as a regular customer!).

→ Gain permission to go into the homes and natural environments of your user/customer/stakeholders to witness firsthand, understand, and inquire about their lifestyle, needs, and values as relevant to what you are designing. This broader context is key to discovering new opportunities.

→ To gain inspiration in a short amount of time, rather than taking the time to survey a large sample, pick a handful of interesting profiles that represent a range of user types (i.e., from existing users and potential future users, to non-users) and spend one to two hours having face-to-face conversations with each person to learn about their lifestyle, needs, and values, which are relevant to what you are designing.

Making a Business Out of Empathic Exercises

"Dining in the Dark" has become a global restaurant phenomenon in which people can experience eating as if they were blind. Not only do you gain empathy for the challenges of being vision impaired, but you can also experience a heightened sensitivity to sounds, touch, tastes, and smells, hosted in a pitch-black dining room, guided by blind servers.

For more info: www.darkdining.com

SEEK OUT ANALOGOUS INSPIRATION

When running an organization or business, it is natural to benchmark yourself against other players in your industry or look within your field for inspiration. Microsoft seeks to steal market share from Apple; McDonald's has to keep an eye on what's going on among other players in the fast-food world; even nations compare their economic and social rankings, learning from global policies and programs. But when it comes to designing future offerings and concepts, focusing solely on one's industry severely limits creativity and innovation.

What serves as fodder for your idea development? What are your "inputs"? Chances are, most of the tradeshows, conferences, and the publications you read tend to be related to your industry. Sure, you need to stay abreast of what your competitors are doing, but most creative thinkers are always seeking out new and diverse experiences in other industry sectors. The more exposure you have to different ideas, experiences, and bodies of knowledge, the easier it is to cross-pollinate ideas and solutions. Contrary to popular belief, most innovations are not created from scratch, but are existing ideas that are borrowed and repurposed or interpreted in a new context.

It's about looking outside your industry to discover unexpected solutions.

When it comes to venturing outside your usual context to gain inspiration that is useful, applicable, and generative, there are different types of inspiration to consider:

- shared context inspiration;

- spin-off inspiration;

- extreme inspiration.

SHARED CONTEXT INSPIRATION

It means becoming inspired by people and processes that share parallel constraints, conditions, or objectives.

 **SURGICAL TEAMS LEARNING FROM RACING PIT CREWS**

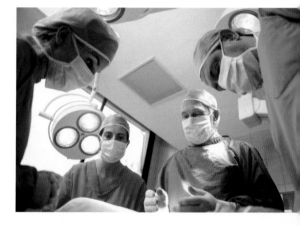

In the search for ways to improve the surgery and recovery process for patients, medical professionals discovered that they had much to learn from race car pit crews who have mastered working under the parallel constraints of intense time pressure, large yet tightly synchronized teams, managing complex procedures and equipment, and trying to minimize errors that can have life or death consequences. Did you know that racing crews can refuel a car and change all four tires in seven seconds, and that no Formula One driver has died at the wheel in a Grand Prix race since 1994? Beyond learning through direct observation of pit crews in action, some hospitals have even engaged racing team members and technical directors to observe their surgical processes and provide on-the-spot opportunities for performance improvement. Specific techniques surgeons, nurses, and other health professionals can adopt from racing crews include how to systematically do high-risk handoffs from one team or site to another, establish role clarity, plan for contingencies, use briefings and checklists to prevent errors, apply technology to transfer key information, and learn post-op procedures by mining data. Teams that adopted racing-inspired processes have reduced their error rates, increased efficiency and communication, and ultimately saved lives. Similarly, the fields of aviation, spaceflight, and the military have also provided inspiration for better ways to manage high-risk procedures.

SPIN-OFF INSPIRATION

It means getting inspired by existing solutions that were invented for a specific application (be they technologies, mechanisms, interactions, or services), to be used in a completely new way or context.

 SPACE TECHNOLOGY ON EARTH

Many composite materials originally developed by NASA to overcome the challenges of operating satellites and spacecraft eventually revolutionize how countless products are made and used here on earth. Industries such as medical, construction, textile, safety, and sports equipment are able to discover and leverage the reflective, fire-retardant, and lightweight yet strong characteristics of composites used in space.

[*Case in Point*] RETHINKING EVERYDAY OBJECTS

When industrial designers were thinking of an ideal interaction to turn on/off a CD player designed for the Japanese home goods brand MUJI, they borrowed from the familiar gesture of tugging on a cord to turn on a light. The result was an unexpected, yet delightfully intuitive way of operating the music player that could be mounted on the wall, unlike most electronics which are variations of black boxed gadgets.

EXTREME INSPIRATION

It means getting inspired by the needs and behaviors of extreme users or extreme contexts of use.

 AERON CHAIR INSPIRED BY THE ELDERLY

The design of the high-end office Aeron Chair was originally intended to serve the heightened ergonomic needs of the elderly which were ill served by conventional furniture. While trying to redesign in-home medical equipment, designers observed how difficult, painful, and uncomfortable it was for elderly patients to use furniture such as the La-Z-Boy recliner style chairs which were often found in hospitals and at home. Understanding (literal as well as metaphorical) pain points allowed them to rethink the fundamental structure of the chair, moving from designing an upholstered wooden box stuffed with foam, to one with flexible fabrics stretched across a plastic frame that was thinner and would mold to the sitter's body and mitigate heat build-up. The concept was actually shelved for years after company founder Herman Miller was unable to find a good way to market furniture for the elderly, but found a second life in adapting the design to targeting the office and workplace market. The Aeron Chair's superior ergonomic qualities, comfort, and radical design also allowed the chair to be positioned as a premium task chair. The key to extreme inspiration is that if a solution serves the needs of extreme users or helps the user to cope with extreme conditions, it is also likely to appeal to users without special needs.

ANALOGOUS INSPIRATION: WHERE TO START...

1

List out central design themes:

Think about the essence of the challenges you are trying to solve. There should be a handful of relevant themes that might deal with environmental, emotional, social, physical, or functional aspects. For example, if you sell cosmetics, some themes might be: making people feel more confident, hiding flaws, experimentation, transformation, playing with different identities, and daily routines. To revisit the pit crew vs. surgical suite example, some themes would be: life and death situations, intense time pressure (seconds count), a plethora of specialized equipment, and a team of multiple experts who need to act in a coordinated fashion. Once you have compiled a list of challenges, it will be easier to brainstorm outside industries or businesses that grapple with the same challenges and obstacles.

2

Brainstorm parallel inspiration:

Think about what other businesses, brands, organizations, products, or contexts share the themes that you've listed. Not all of the parallels have to be compatible with each theme; there can be different examples for different themes. Racing pit crews may offer speed and efficiency ideas, airline crews may provide safety ideas, and military SWAT teams may lend team communication or leadership ideas. The key is to consider which analogous context has solutions that you can learn from or adopt, and are relevant yet different from what your industry typically does.

3

Observe and experience for yourself:

Get out there and observe these parallel inspirations in practice! That is the best way to learn about how different contexts are approaching the design challenge you face. Observe solutions in action, interview people and experts in different industries, and walk through analogous experiences with fresh eyes. For the medical example, you would gain the most by getting to observe the pit crews in action, interviewing technical managers, getting to see the actual tools, workflows, and practices they use to maintain their standards and results first hand, as it happens, rather than just reading about it or watching it on TV.

SOLVE PROBLEMS WITH INTERDISCIPLINARY TEAMS

Typically within organizations, the generation of new ideas is a task assigned to a specific group such as R&D, product development, or disciplines such as engineering or marketing. However, this leaves a great deal of unlocked innovation potential. When creativity or idea development is done exclusively by one camp, conflict arises at each handover due to different agendas and areas of focus from one siloed group to the next.

Solving tough challenges requires tapping into the collective wisdom of people with different perspectives. For example, a marketer may be better at managing communications and media, while a frontline service representative understands customer demands, an engineer knows how to build tangible solutions, and a manager may understand how to navigate internal processes and politics. All these areas of expertise are critical to the eventual implementation and success of an idea.

In short, having a more open, interdisciplinary approach will yield stronger, more varied and viable ideas and also nurture people and organizational cultures to be more collaborative and innovative. Encouraging more diverse voices to collaborate earlier in the process may require more work in the beginning, but the resulting ideas will be more holistic, feasible, and have a better chance of succeeding in the long run.

INTERDISCIPLINARY TEAMS:
WHERE TO START...

Whenever you can, create a "dream team" that collaborates early in the ideation process.

Choose individuals who:

→ can speak to different aspects of your value chain (from development to implementation and beyond). This ensures that you develop an idea that will consider opportunities and barriers throughout the life cycle of your offering.

→ have diverse expertise/backgrounds. If everyone thinks/acts/looks the same you need more diversity.

→ are positive, productive, and team players by nature. Upstream idea creation is NOT the time for feasibility-obsessed, nit-picky, and overly critical voices. These attitudes will severely hinder the creative process, stifle ideas, and cripple your team's morale.

PROTOTYPING TO LEARN: HOW TO DO IT

Almost anything can be prototyped, using simple and low-cost methods.

- **Interactions:** Rather than spending hours coding and programming early ideas which will surely change, use fast and easy materials like paper and sketches to mock up ideas and applications.

- **Services:** Services may be intangible, but can be tested and developed using role-playing, simulations, and props.

- **Spaces:** Before you invest millions, build temporary structures using cardboard or cheap materials in a warehouse or empty space to see how different spatial concepts feel and could be used.

- **Products:** Use cheap craft materials to play with different forms and detailed aspects of how the user may use and interact with the product and its features.

- **Communication:** In today's digital age, it has never been easier to create quick visual mock-ups (ads, websites, and marketing material) and place them in different contexts to test how different communications are perceived by your intended audience. Computer-aided design programs can also help you to produce quick, highly inventive on-screen mockups.

- **Processes:** Bring together communications, products, space, and service prototypes to test holistic experiments in action.

PROTOTYPING TO LEARN: IMPORTANT TIPS

When ideas are at an early stage...

- Prototypes don't need to be perfect. Make them "quick and rough." In fact, if they are too perfect, you are probably over-invested in an idea at too early a stage to know if it's the right one.

- Mock ideas up in full size so that people can interact and play with them in a realistic context.

- Keep things rough and simple and focus on representing the intended experience and interactions—the feel and intent rather than the look and aesthetic.

- Don't be afraid of showing imperfect ideas as work in progress. Explain to people that your objective is to get feedback to improve the concept early rather than late. If people are used to seeing "perfect examples or proposals", discuss the benefits of and philosophy behind the prototyping approach ahead of time (i.e. "This will save our company time and money in the long run").

- Don't get too attached to one idea. Make a series of prototypes or make them modular so that you can test out multiple ideas or variations. Chances are, the "right idea" will end up being an amalgamation of the strongest features or ideas.

ADDRESSING REAL-WORLD TENSIONS THROUGH THE TAO

Chapter 4 thus far draws largely on the methodology of design thinking for generating new ideas and solutions. I suggested strategies to generate meaningful human-centered idea creation by applying user empathy, analogous inspiration, interdisciplinary problem-solving, and experimentation using prototyping to learn. However, this contradicts the more commonly used analytical and data-driven market research practices, which follow a more linear process of defining a solution, then testing to predict the potential success of that pre-defined solution.

As you answer this chapter's innovation question, "How do you move beyond the status quo?," be prepared to face tension between the values of:

DATA VS. EXPERIENCE

Data and statistics are the basis of most quantitative market research, which is used to help organizations converge quickly on specific ideas or provide a high-level summary. The conventional practice begins with looking at creating an improved product idea through engineering solutions and then using quantitative "new product concept testing" market research to verify the extent of "believability," "desirability," and "intent to purchase" among target customers.

Another side of qualitative research examines the human experience to inspire and inform the development of meaningful new offerings. It is just as important for innovators to use human-centered design thinking methods to understand users and the people that will be engaged in creating a product or offering. Tapping into people's values, aspirations, and latent or unarticulated needs can reveal opportunities that data-driven competitors overlook. This process can be more diffused, divergent, and intuitive in nature, looking beyond conventional boundaries and typically making data-driven companies very uncomfortable. It requires a few cycles of diverging and converging to test and fine-tune ideas as more insight is gained.

RECONCILING THE TENSION

To reconcile the tension between what statistics show and what experience shows, you need to:

Diverge in order to better converge.

The process of front-end innovation is an iterative process of refinement and prototyping of ideas. The rapid pace of today's corporate and entrepreneurial environment frequently causes innovators and new product development managers to converge on the specifics of an idea too quickly, using only quantitative market research data without going through the necessary experimental iterations to fine-tune and test ideas sufficiently with a diffused set of target customers before going to market. The way to reconcile this is to understand that to derive the best possible new product idea in the shortest possible time, you have to diverge and converge repeatedly along the process of idea creation, so that you can meaningfully address your customers' aspirations, values, and unmet needs.

Quantitative market research methodologies should be combined with creative design thinking practices. You should first go through the human-centered, front-end innovation process to get inspired and identify potential new products, services, and offerings. Then use more conventional hard-core quantitative market research to validate your ideas and understand how to make the target customers value them, desire them, and decide to purchase them. Conventional quantitative data can be used to estimate the product adoption rate more effectively at product launch and can then be adjusted along the way. Once your innovation is out in the real world, allow real-time market and customer adoption feedback to closely guide its evolution and test your business model hypotheses.

How do you move beyond the status quo?

Answering this question starts with the practice of:

Inspiring Breakthrough Ideas

▼ Identify the most significant pain points along your customer's journey by doing some "empathic exercises."

▼ Reflect on how other organizations, businesses, or brands outside your industry have successfully addressed the common challenges you face.

▼ Recruit other disciplines upstream that add a valuable perspective and make your team more diverse.

▼ What ideas are you most excited about? Start prototyping those and gain feedback by testing them in quick and rough ways.

Want to go deeper?

Further Reading

Kelley, T. and Littman, J. (2001). *The art of innovation*. New York, NY: Currency/Doubleday.

Kelley, T. and Littman, J. (2005). *The ten faces of innovation: IDEO's strategies for defeating the devil's advocate and driving creativity throughout your organization.* New York, NY: Currency/Doubleday.

Video: Design & Thinking—a documentary on design thinking [Video file]. Retrieved from http://www.designthinkingmovie.com.

How do you put yourself in the right place at the right time?

Water symbolizes "the way" to answer this question.

Water FLOWS. This element teaches us to go with the current, not against it.

Water represents the practice of Riding the Waves of Opportunity.

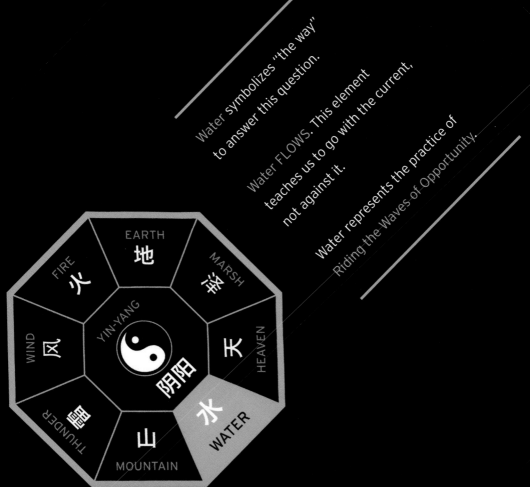

EARTH
地

MARSH
沢

FIRE
火

HEAVEN
天

YIN-YANG
阴阳

WIND
风

WATER
水

THUNDER
雷

MOUNTAIN
山

How do you put yourself in the right place at the right time?

WHY IS THIS QUESTION IMPORTANT?

Success does not occur accidentally but is driven by changing market forces and other conditions. If you introduce your innovation when there is no driving market force, it will likely fail. You need to time the roll out of your innovation, so that it is riding the headwinds of strong market trends and profits shifts.

"You cannot direct the wind. But you can adjust your sails." –German proverb

*I*t is not enough to have a great idea. Many great ideas failed because they were ahead of their time or a little too far behind. An innovation's success largely depends on whether market forces are in its favor at the time of its release. Is the consumer and market infrastructure ready for the idea? Are market forces ripe to accelerate its adoption? History shows that opportunities to profit tend to occur in predictable patterns. These profit patterns describe different ways value migrates from antiquated business designs to new, innovative ones that address new and emerging customer priorities. Experienced business innovators who learn how to recognize and anticipate the emergence of profit patterns will succeed if they prepare, change, and innovate their business design models ahead of the competition; if they are out in front.

This chapter is about learning how to recognize emerging profit patterns that may be occurring in your industry. Adrian Slywotzky and David Morrison pioneered the concept of identifying patterns within major profit opportunities in their book, Profit Patterns (1999). Slywotzky, creator of the term "demand innovation" discussed in Chapter 3, describes more than 30 important profit patterns he identified during his business research into over 200 companies in 40 diverse industries. These profit patterns emerged for many different reasons and were triggered by various conditions. No single condition will trigger a profit pattern. Usually, multiple elements combine to foster the emergence of a new pattern. As innovators, it is important to figure out which profit patterns you can exploit to help propel your innovation to success. This chapter introduces the six major profit patterns that Slywotzky suggests are the mega patterns most relevant to innovators and ways to profit from emerging profit patterns.

STEPS FOR YOUR ACTION PLAN

Review these profit patterns in relation to your industry:

1. No profit
2. Back to profit
3. Convergence
4. Redefinition
5. Channel compression
6. Technology shifts the board

WHAT THEY HELP YOU ACCOMPLISH

Recognizing which profit pattern affects your industry can help you to anticipate opportunities

PROFIT PATTERN **1** NO PROFIT

This is when once profitable businesses become unprofitable, which causes the entire industry to suffer. It occurs when too many businesses compete, using a similar business design. This creates market conditions in which everyone competes in the same way, which ultimately leads to price erosion and commoditization of products and services—wherein products that were in some way differentiated from each other are viewed by the consumer as the same or not unique—and a loss of the industry's cumulative profit pool.

[*Case in Point*] THE AIRLINE INDUSTRY

In 1978, the US Airline Deregulation Act of 1978 removed government control over commercial airline fares, routes, and requirements for market entry of new airlines. As a result, in the 1980s, the airline industry attracted many new companies to enter the business, which intensified competition. Most airline companies such as United, Delta, and US Air competed using a similar business model: purchasing many different types of airplanes for different routes and flight distances, using large network computers to book flight reservations, selling tickets through travel agents, offering in-flight food service, and using the hub-and-spoke flight scheduling network (e.g., all flights leave from and return to the main airline hub). Most major airlines adopted these expensive service offerings and bundles which caused them to be viewed as undifferentiated by the consumer, ultimately leading to price competition and the erosion of cumulative industry profit to zero by the early 1990s.

How to Profit

Walk away or invent a new way of doing business. For example, Southwest Airlines uses a point-to-point flight network (i.e., not always returning to a hub) with shorter flight routes but more frequent flights, only flies fuel-efficient 737 jets (thus simplifying maintenance requirements), offers no-frills service on board to cut costs, and offers passenger self-check-in service.

PROFIT PATTERN ② BACK TO PROFIT

The back to profit pattern occurs when a novel business design emerges to make an industry profitable again. The coffee industry, watch making, and grocery distribution businesses have seen profits bounce back due to business design innovation brought about by companies such as Starbucks, Swatch Watch, and Whole Foods respectively.

[*Case in Point*] STARBUCKS VS. THE REST OF THE COFFEE INDUSTRY

Coffee sold through grocery stores has been a profitless item for most fast-moving consumer product companies like Folgers (P&G), Maxwell House (General Foods), and Nestlé (Nestlé). Supermarkets treat coffee as a loss leader item but stock it to attract customers to purchase other breakfast items such as orange juice, bread, cereal, and milk. Massive TV advertising to promote the brand promotes sales and intensifies competition, but also erodes industry profits and turns the instant coffee business into an undifferentiated commodity.

The rapid growth of Starbucks throughout the 1990s redefined coffee from being viewed simply as a beverage to a cultural experience. The company positioned coffee as an "affordable luxury." Starbucks coffee shops are viewed by many customers as the "third place" to spend time, after their home and office. Starbucks succeeded without the use of 60-second advertising, which was the core promotion strategy of most coffee businesses that wanted to move their products quickly through highly competitive national and regional grocery stores.

Instead, Starbucks has been highly effective by extending its brand into selling different coffee products such as ice creams, coffee beans, instant coffee, and canned iced coffee in supermarkets, restaurants, airlines, kiosks, and other high-margin channels of distribution. Starbucks' new and highly differentiated business design model created a new format for retailing coffee beverages, which is highly profitable, both nationally and globally. This innovative coffee beverage business has caused a significant stock value migration away from the old traditional coffee business. Starbucks has created more than $56.14 billion in shareholder value through its market capitalization by mid-2014.

How to Profit

Ask yourself, "How much variation in customer needs exists in my market? What are my target customers' most undiscovered and unarticulated needs that have significant market potential?" Then build a new and innovative business design to meet these needs.

PROFIT PATTERN ③ CONVERGENCE

Convergence is triggered by a change in the industry, such as the advent of a new technology (e.g., cloud computing), or a change in legislation, after which the rules of competition are forever changed. As a result, industries that were previously focused on one area can now enter into other business sectors, and vice versa. This convergence of business boundaries, where two to three or more industries can be combined and rolled up together, causes traditional barriers and market boundaries to collapse. You see con-vergence occur on many different levels, in products and services, in whole industries, and with materials. When industry or product convergence happens, the new converged market can be more than 10 times larger than the original individual market. The Internet revolution and the computing power advances in the last 20 years are the main trigger for convergence as witnessed in industries such as financial services, health care, computing and information, and biomedical engineering.

[*Case in Point*]

PRODUCT/SERVICE CONVERGENCE: THE CELL PHONE

The cellular phone's original purpose was to allow users to make and receive calls. However, technology changed and improved, and now the cell phone has become a smartphone. It connects us to the Internet, serves as a social media hub, takes photos and videos, sends email and social media, plays music, stores games, allows us to pay bills and purchase products and services, keeps our calendars, and has countless other mobile applications. The cell phone is an example of how various products and services can be provided by one device and of a technological application revolution.

[*Case in Point*]

WHOLE INDUSTRY: BANKING

The banking industry has seen significant industry convergence. Banks were traditionally places to store money safely and to apply for loans. However, when banking became deregulated, banks began offering a whole suite of financial services: you can invest in mutual funds and stocks, buy insurance, get personal financial investment advice, do mobile banking, and more.

The steel industry underwent major convergence as well. In the 1960s, steel was the lead material in cars, making them strong, but also very heavy. Within 30 years, however, plastic and aluminum production became more efficient and accessible and technological advancements occurred to make them cheaper and stronger. Today, most car parts are made with plastic and aluminum because they are lighter than steel. Now cars are composed of less than 50% steel, and that proportion will continue to decrease over time. Note that no steel company chose to create a hybrid material to rival the increasing domination of major plastics and aluminum producers—so their market share and profits (from cars) were diminishing more and more. The plastic and aluminum producers emerged as the winners of materials convergence.

How to Profit

When convergence occurs, market opportunities can increase exponentially. Companies that can adapt quickly and reorganize to compete in the new convergence market with new rules can benefit by carving out a place in a much larger and more complex market. Companies need to look beyond their traditional boundaries in the new opportunity for convergence and redefine their business definitions.

Ask yourself, is the convergence pattern happening in your industry? Are your adjacent industries growing more rapidly than and drawing profit away from yours? Then construct a View of the Future, lay new bets about your industry, looking 5 to 10 years ahead, and anticipate which new trends may emerge. How can you create new sources of revenue to exploit the new trends?

PROFIT PATTERN **4** REDEFINITION

This pattern occurs when you redefine what constitutes your customer base. New opportunities arise when a new and different customer group with new aspirations and motivations, new influences, new customer behavior and buying habits come into play in an existing industry. Your company may face saturation of your customer base and you may not recognize a new important segment of customers emerging, with new aspirations and needs that your business is not prepared to meet–yet. The shift from old and established customers to new and untapped ones presents a profit opportunity that your company should be prepared to exploit.

 **BANG AND OLUFSEN**

Bang and Olufsen (B&O), a Danish high-end consumer electronics company, suffered from profit stagnation in the 1980s. Its traditional customers were knowledgeable audiophiles who appreciated the fine details of their stereo systems, including sophisticated engineering and improved sound quality in B&O products. The company redefined its traditional niche customer base and decided to shift to the luxury-seeking segment, which appreciates elegance, prestige, and status symbols as much as sleek design and fine engineering. The new B&O focused on aesthetics, styling, and design of B&O products' appearance, not just on technical and performance aspects; a reflection of the targeted consumer's sophisticated taste. B&O's new strategy increased its share value to revenue ratio from 0.2 in 1989 to 1.5 times in 1997 when most consumer electronics firms hovered in the 0.5 range. This means that for every dollar of sales B&O generated its stock value was actually worth $1.5, far higher than that of their competitors.

How to Profit

Look beyond your current traditional customer group and monitor current and potential competitors. Search adjacent markets and industries for profitable customer segments and alter your business design to attract them. Ask yourself how many of your competitors are redefining their customers and competitive landscape? Are other companies outside your industry redefining their traditional customers and stealing your most profitable customer groups?

PROFIT PATTERN ⑤ CHANNEL COMPRESSION

Channel compression occurs when multi-step distribution systems are compressed by reducing the number of intermediaries or steps needed to reach their end consumer. For example, the digital revolution has displaced multi-step distribution channel systems in which wholesaler, regional distributors, dealers, and retailers historically functioned to break bulk purchases down and distribute products to end users. These traditional three-to-four-step distribution processes are very costly and lack efficiency due to a long distribution cycle and lack of customer responsiveness. Similarly, new businesses that use the Internet for mass customization and direct, one-to-one, real-time, on-demand marketing have forged direct relationships between suppliers and end users, cutting out one or more middle men (disintermediation).

[*Case in Point*] CALYX AND COROLLA

A classic example is Calyx and Corolla, the San Francisco-based direct online flower company, which anticipated the channel compression/disintermediation approach by determining the key pain points and dysfunctional distribution network between flower growers and distributors. The company saw profits being eaten up by the seasonal availability and perishable nature of flowers sold through traditional independent brick and mortar flower shops and supermarkets; flowers took 7 to 10 days to go from farm to store.

Ruth Owades, founder of Calyx and Corolla, worked very closely with growers to develop packaging materials that would keep flowers moist and fresh longer and formed an alliance with Federal Express to ship flowers directly to consumers, bypassing the traditional middleman. Channel compression and disintermediation eliminated low-value-added distributors and formed direct links between suppliers and customers. As a result, costs were reduced, capital and assets also greatly decreased, and the quality of the product and information flow between suppliers and customers greatly improved. Calyx and Corolla removed unnecessary steps in the flower distribution system, streamlined delivery, and improved customer satisfaction by lowering purchasing costs and improving the quality and freshness of flowers.

A more modern example is the effect that Amazon.com, the US-based e-commerce company, has had on the book industry. Amazon.com effectively eliminated the middleman–physical bookstores–replacing them with direct one-to-one marketing for new and used books. Rather than shipping books to stores, the company ships them directly from the warehouse at much lower cost. It eventually began offering other e-commence consumer product merchandise such as toys, shoes, clothing, and electronics.

PROFIT PATTERN 6 TECHNOLOGY SHIFTS THE BOARD

This pattern occurs when a new technological development pushes traditional players out of their accustomed positions. Technology shifts allow for rapid redistribution of power between supplier, partners, agents, distributors, buyers, customers, and end users. This has a significant impact on the competitive landscape and increases opportunities for profitable and purposeful innovation. The advent of digital technology, computing, and the Internet are the three most powerful drivers of this profit pattern.

How to Profit

Ask yourself what competitive advantages your business has over your competitors in manufacturing and buying operations. Can you create more direct links upstream or downstream in the distribution chain? Can you eliminate low-value-added steps or create new value-added offerings in your distribution systems to get closer to the end users more efficiently and economically?

In the finance world, Yuebao (余额宝), an online investment product offered since 2013 through the Chinese e-commerce giant Alibaba Group Holding Ltd's third-party payment affiliate, Alipay, has completely reinvented investment funds for everyday people in a market dominated by state-owned banks. Yuebao, which translates into "leftover treasure," allows users of Alipay (similar to PayPal in the United States) to put the unused balance in their accounts into investments funds with no minimum amount and to withdraw it at any time without penalty. Alipay then aggregates and invests the balance, which would otherwise be lying idle. Users can also realize short-term gains from these "micro-investments." In its first year, Yuebao was able to offer an annual interest rate of around 6% (compared to major bank rates of 0.35%).

The Internet has created huge advantages for online banks over their traditional brick and mortar counterparts, mainly due to drastically lower overheads and infrastructure costs. Alibaba, Alipay's holding company, also owns China's largest e-commerce platform, Taobao, and other e-commerce subsidiaries, presenting endless possibilities for leveraging customer and financial data across their businesses to create innovative products and services for its 800+ million registered users. Within nine months of its inception, Yuebao became China's largest online money market fund, attracting more than 81 million investors, more than those in all of China's equity markets. As of March 2014, Yuebao had accumulated more than 500 billion yuan ($81 billion) in deposits. Yuebao is paving the way for a huge uptake of online investing in China and poses a significant challenge to traditional retail banking products.

How to Profit

Ask yourself whether there are there any emerging technology shift patterns that will alter the dynamics of power and relationships between players in your industry. Who will benefit the most from the technology shift? The customers? Suppliers? Industry players? Who will be hurt the most? Go to where the power lies. What can you do to benefit from shifts in technology and minimize any negative impact on your company?

So far Chapter 5 is about finding the most opportune time to launch a new product or service idea. Innovators will have an uphill battle to create strong market forces if they have to start from scratch. An innovation has a better chance of gaining momentum and traction if it can ride on the waves of some emerging profit patterns, which can propel a well-thought-out new product idea into a solid product. An organization may even be able to ride on multiple profit patterns. When this occurs, success is usually astronomical. Profit patterns can help you understand when the market and consumer conditions are most conducive for your innovation. The challenge is one of timing—whether your product will be ready when market forces are most advantageous for its release. Product launch dates are typically driven, not by when the market is ready, but on development schedules, budgets, performance targets, earnings reports, etc.—by interior, not exterior factors.

As you answer this chapter's innovation question, "How do you put yourself in the right place at the right time?," be prepared to face tension between the values of:

PRODUCT READINESS VS **MARKET READINESS**

Product readiness is when your ideas have reached an ideal state of maturity, have resulted in a tangible, marketable product, and are ready for commercialization. Your innovation has gone through all your organization's due processes and checks to create a complete combination of product, service, and marketing.

Market readiness requires you to wait (or sometimes speed up) processes so that all market forces and powerful profit pattern(s) align before product launch.

To reconcile the tension between how ready your product is versus how ripe the market is, you need to:

Combine a new product innovation with an innovative business design that rides on waves of positive market forces and multiple profit patterns.

Having only a well-researched and well-thought-out product is insufficient. It needs to be aligned with powerful market forces. The exercise of analyzing profit patterns should occur upfront during product idea creation and design so that when the product design is ready to launch, the launch date allows it to ride on the waves of positive market forces and powerful profit patterns.

$$\left[\ \mathscr{Case\ in\ Point}\ \right]\quad \text{XIAOMI}$$

Xiaomi is a mobile Internet startup-turned-superstar company, known for reinventing the smartphone business model in the world's largest market—China. It only took three short years since its inception in 2010 for Xiaomi to overtake Apple in 2013 to become China's third largest smartphone supplier, behind Samsung and ZTE. The company sold 18.7 million smartphones in 2013, generating a revenue of almost US$5.2 billion, representing 150% growth in that year.

Xiaomi is both a hardware and software company, selling its own highly customizable Android-based MIUI firmware, the platform on which its smartphones are built. It uses its hardware to create a robust software platform riding on the power of the Internet, e-commerce, and apps. Its users have downloaded more than a billion paid apps, games, advertising, and other fee-based services. For example, its music platform, i.xiaomi.com, allows independent musicians to upload their songs and charge whatever price they wish with all the proceeds going to the musician for the first two years. Xiaomi's e-commerce platform is already the third largest in China. In 2014, Xiaomi entered into a strategic partnership with Beijing Bank to promote mobile banking and finance including features such as mobile payment and credit card services, microfinance, and mobile financial management services, such as selling mutual funds and insurance through phones. The company is said to have a valuation of $10 billion, on par with Lenovo and twice BlackBerry's valuation in late 2013.

From 2010, when the company entered the market, to 2013, it has grown rapidly, riding on the waves of multiple profit patterns such as:

- Technology shifts across the board: Xiaomi entered the market as a late-comer, but it took advantage of the advent of Internet technologies such as cloud computing, computing speed and storage capacity, the open Android operating system, and the digital revolution to build its robust software platform and coordinate it with its existing hardware. Every Tuesday at noon Beijing time, the company ships a new batch of phones, influenced strongly by user feedback to determine what changes it should make. The close connection with its users on forums and rapid design development cycle allows it to add new software and even hardware tweaks in its weekly shipments, which is truly unique in the mobile market.

- Product/industry convergence: Although smartphones and e-commerce are overcrowded, red ocean markets, Xiaomi's innovative business design model rides on the wave of rapid product and market convergence. The smartphone has now become a mobile phone, a digital camera, a mobile personal computer, an electronic wallet and financial services center, a virtual market place, a personal navigator, a games and entertainment center, and a networking and social media hub. Industry profit pools are reshuffled and relocated in different profit zones when convergence takes place, creating an industry that is exponentially larger than the original stand-alone cell phone market. With expertise in both hardware and software development, Xiaomi has great advantages over other mobile players.

- No-profit to profit: The mobile phone business is a high-volume, low-margin business. Many hardware manufacturers suffer from selling unprofitable handsets. Xiaomi's unique e-commerce business model allows it to use its hardware to develop a software platform to monetize its e-commerce, apps, and mobile finance and banking businesses. At the same time, it is able to sell its most affordable models for one-third of the price of an Apple iPhone, which makes these products much more accessible and attractive to most Chinese consumers.

How do you put yourself in the right place at the right time?

Answering this question starts with the practice of:

Riding the Waves of Opportunity

▼ Review the profit patterns in the chapter and identify the profit patterns that are affecting your current industry. If none of them apply, you can learn about other profit patterns in the further reading section.

▼ Create a strategy to exploit the profit pattern trend for your business.

Want to go deeper?

Further Reading

Slywotzky, A. and Morrison, D. (1999). *Profit patterns*. New York, NY: Times Business.

CHAPTER 6   MOUNTAIN 山

How do you craft a strong and lasting go-to-market strategy?

Mountain symbolizes "the way" to answer this question.

Mountain GROUNDS you. It has majestic stability and strength. This element teaches us to build a strong foundation that can last through time.

Mountain represents the practice of Building the Master Plan.

How do you craft a strong and lasting go-to-market strategy?

WHY IS THIS QUESTION IMPORTANT?

To succeed in business, you need a solid go-to-market master plan to roll out your venture idea. Your business master plan serves as a blueprint for how you intend to get your offering to your user and generate adoption and wealth. This master plan needs to be carefully conceived to reduce the risk of failure and sustain your competitive advantage in the market.

A business master plan represents the formulation of your entire business strategy to help realize your vision or dream. This formulation must be carefully conceived because the overall strategy has significant implications for every aspect of your business. I like to use the analogy that building a master business plan is like building a house that has three basic stages: (1) laying the foundation, which needs to be strong and stable, (2) developing the floor plan, which needs to be functional and flow well, and (3) creating the construction schedule, which needs to stay on time and on budget.

Analogously, the development of a winning, strategic business master plan is very similar to the three-step approach to building a house. A master plan consists of the following three parts:

Part **1** A **business design**, similar to an architectural plan, laying out the foundation and structural plan of a house. The business design describes the core strategy and core foundation of a new or future business and how it will sustain its competitive advantage over long periods of time.

Part **2** A **business model**, which is like the layout of your house, such as where the living room will be compared to the kitchen. Your business model must describe the operational tactics; how the various components of running your business will work together to implement your business design. It should be adaptive enough to respond to changing market conditions and must be constantly reviewed and renewed to create the differentiation needed to support your unique value proposition.

Part **3** A **business plan**, much like a building construction plan detailing the start to finish of a project. The business plan should be aligned closely to your business design and business model to provide timely execution of your innovation and to prepare the company for scaling when your innovation's adoption rate takes off rapidly.

Over the years, I have learned about several important tools that can help you to clearly think through and articulate your business master plan, and most importantly, make it a successful and long-lasting business innovation plan.

STEPS FOR YOUR ACTION PLAN	WHAT THEY HELP YOU ACCOMPLISH
Define your business design	Describe your fundamental business assumptions and critical strategic platforms that will drive your innovations
Redesign your business model	Identify how the nine fundamental elements of your current business model will be different in your business model redesign
Create a business plan	Develop an integrated business plan that can be used to seek funding and resource support

The hierarchy of levels of importance in the strategy formulation process from most important (base of the pyramid) to least important (top of the pyramid) are:

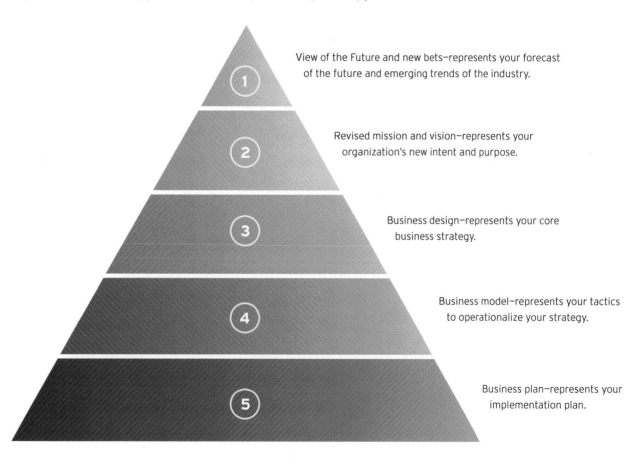

View of the Future and new bets—represents your forecast of the future and emerging trends of the industry.

Revised mission and vision—represents your organization's new intent and purpose.

Business design—represents your core business strategy.

Business model—represents your tactics to operationalize your strategy.

Business plan—represents your implementation plan.

Part 1

DEFINE YOUR BUSINESS DESIGN: YOUR FOUNDATION

When you build a house, an architect must prepare a structural plan for the foundation. The foundation must be able to support the size of the house, protect against outside elements such as water from entering the house, and withstand the structural beams and load-bearing thrust and pillars needed to support the overall weight and construction. The parallel in innovation is to prepare a business design to, first, help define your fundamental business assumption and, second, define the strategic, operational, and organizational platforms needed to help propel your innovation and sustain your competitive advantage over time. We use an approach to craft a winning business design defined by Adrian J. Slywotzky and David J. Morrison in their books, *Value Migration* (1996) and *Profit Zone* (1997), to show how to design strategies to challenge traditional models of competition. Slywotzky, an economic theorist and management guru who has written several books on profitability and growth, pioneered the concept of business design and business model innovation helping many firms look beyond just focusing on products and services, to address the underlying design of the business.

How to Construct a Business Design

Business design is the process of formulating your core strategies to support your View of the Future and bets. Slywotzky suggests a three-step approach to construct an innovative business design:

Step 1 Define your business fundamental assumptions.

Step 2 Define the strategic, organizational, and operational platforms of your new or future business.

Step 3 Define how your business design differs from that of your key competitor.

step

Define Your Business's Fundamental Assumptions

The fundamental assumption that your business is based on forms the core strategy of your innovation. It explicitly depicts the mental model of your value proposition and how it will attract customers from other alternatives in the market. Just as how you build the foundation of a house is determined by various factors (e.g., size, the type of soil on which it is built, the climate, the direction the house is facing), the foundation of your business fundamental assumption should be well informed by your View of the Future, the bets you laid, and your new mission and vision. Slywotzky cited the coffee business and the plastics and aluminum vs. steel businesses to explain the differentiation of fundamental assumptions between two different business designs competing in the same industry.

In 1987, three major coffee brands in the US market, Folgers (Proctor & Gamble), Maxwell House (General Foods), and Nestlé held over 90% of over $1 billion in shareholder value in the coffee industry, mostly selling pre-ground vacuum-sealed coffee. By the mid 1990s gourmet coffee roasters (e.g., Millstone, Green Coffee Association, Chock full o'Nuts) were offering high-quality Arabica whole bean coffee, freshly roasted, which resulted in cafés and espresso stands popping up all over street corners across America. Starbucks had close to 50 stores in 1989 and by 1999 Starbucks had grown rapidly to almost 2,500 stores globally. The three major traditional brands were still selling low-quality, vacuum-packed, ground coffee through groceries stores. Their market share and shareholder value tumbled to levels below revenue. During that 10-year period, customer priorities had shifted from low price, ease of purchase, and a uniform offering, to new priorities around quality, freshness, proximity to office, and experiencing a growing coffee culture.

Business fundamental assumptions for traditional coffee business design (Folgers, Maxwell House, Nestlé):

- Coffee is coffee, coffee is just a commodity.

- We need to focus on mass-produced, pre-ground, and vacuum-packed coffee because consumers are not willing to pay for a premium, ground coffee.

- We need to compete on lower costs. Branding via lots of advertising is the key differentiator.

VS.

Business fundamental assumptions for premium coffee business design (Starbucks, Seattle's Best, Tully Coffee):

- Coffee can be an affordable luxury and lifestyle.

- Customers will pay for high-quality premium coffee sold through cafés.

- A coffee culture can be cultivated to create loyal customers in a sophisticated environment.

After the Great Depression and the post-World War II era, the 1950s and 1960s were periods during which integrated steel mills in the United States underwent huge growth and profitability. Automakers and appliance manufacturers, such as General Electric and Westinghouse, as well as construction firms and canning companies, were all on a great growth trajectory. At that time, US steel mills were pursuing vertical integration to achieve low cost and maximum manufacturing efficiency. Customers did not have other substitutable material choices or the option of purchasing from low-cost foreign competitors. Most of the large steel companies were using basic blast furnaces with high fixed costs and low incremental costs, as opposed to electric arc furnaces used to make steel for scrap materials. The estimated market value of the eight American integrated steel mills in the 1960s was approximately $55 billion. However, by 1993, the market value of the surviving integrated steel mill shrank to only $13 billion. Value originally captured by this business design had begun to migrate toward four other business designs more closely aligned to changing customer priorities. The four other competitive business designs were:

1. low-cost foreign mills that used flat-rolled steel,

2. mini mills that used non-flat-rolled applications,

3. aluminum for canning and other applications, and

4. plastic for auto applications.

Lightweight and corrosion resistance had also become new customer priorities rather than structural functionality and meeting minimum quality thresholds.

Below is a comparison of the business design fundamental assumptions of the three different types of steel mills in competition.

Business fundamental assumptions for US Integrated Mills:

- The vertically integrated, blast furnace, basic oxygen steelmaking method is the only way to produce low-cost steel at high speed, despite resulting in plants that are large and asset-intensive.

VS.

Business fundamental assumptions for Japanese Integrated Mills

- A quality, low-cost product will gain customers and acceptance.

- A continuous casting production method can be achieved at economies of scale.

VS.

Business fundamental assumptions for Mini-Mills:

- Steel can be made economically in small quantities using an electric arc furnace.

- The plants are asset-efficient and small. Customers will accept scrap steel as raw materials for lower-end steel products.

These examples illustrate the direct effects that your business fundamental assumptions have on your strategy and ability to compete and respond to changing customer priorities. As the core strategy, it is perhaps the most important thing you need to do after you develop your View of the Future and lay bets.

step

Build Out Your Strategic, Operational, and Organizational Platforms

Once you have outlined your business fundamental assumption, you need to think through three distinct key platforms based on your strategy, operations, and organization. Under each of these platforms are specific critical dimensions that require you to make focused choices. The following is a list of some of the key dimensions within each platform and some of the questions to ask yourself to determine how you will operationalize your organization's fundamental assumption. You may have more dimensions to add that are relevant to your industry or organization.

KEY QUESTIONS

FUNDAMENTAL ASSUMPTION

Based on: How are my customers changing? What are customers' priorities? What are the profit drivers for the business?

STRATEGIC DIMENSIONS

Customer Selection

To which customers can I add real value? Which customers allow me to profit? Which customers do I not want to serve?

Value Capture

How do I recapture a portion of the value created for customers as profit? What is my profit model?

Differentiation / Strategic Control

Why do my chosen customers buy from me? What makes my value proposition unique from those of my competitors? What strategic control points can counterbalance customer power?

Scope

What products/services do I want to sell? Which support activities do I want to perform in-house? Which ones do I want to subcontract or outsource?

OPERATING DIMENSIONS	KEY QUESTIONS
Purchasing System	How do I buy? Transactional or long-term relationship? Antagonistic or partnership?
Manufacturing / Operating Systems	How much do I manufacture versus subcontract? Are my manufacturing/service delivery economics based primarily on fixed or variable costs? Do I need state-of-the-art or 90th-percentile process technology?
Capital Intensity	Do I choose a capital-intensive, high-fixed-cost operating system? Or a less capital-intensive flexible approach?
R&D / Product Development	Internal or outsourced? Focused on process or product? Focused on astute project selection? Speed of development?
Go-to-market Mechanism	Direct sales force? Low-cost distribution? Account management? Licensing? Hybrid?

ORGANIZATIONAL DIMENSIONS	
Organizational Configuration	Centralized or decentralized? Pyramid or network? Functional, business, or matrixed?
Hiring	Internal promotion or external hiring?
Incentive	Fixed or variable or mixed? Equity?

Source: From The Profit Zone by Adrian Slywotzky, David Morrison, and Bob Andelman, copyright © 1997. Used with permission of Random House.

As you create the business design of your organization, thinking through your fundamental assumption and key platforms, you need to also consider the same factors for your competitors. By doing so, you can map out and understand how your business resembles but also differs from your competitors', and identify your competitive edge. The best way to explain how to complete Steps 1 to 3 of the business design is with an example.

[*Case in Point*] WHOLE FOODS VS. SAFEWAY GROCERY CHAINS

This case exemplifies the importance and impact of a strong business design. Whole Foods, Inc., a premium natural foods grocery chain across North America, has successfully competed against traditional grocery chains such as Safeway, Inc. (the second largest grocer in America) because it has a highly differentiated and innovative business design.

Whole Foods' fundamental assumption is that people are willing to pay a premium for organic, natural, sustainably sourced foods, whereas most national grocers, such as Safeway, assume that lower price and value, variety, and accessibility are the most important features of grocery distribution. Whole Foods' philosophy is "Whole Food, Whole People, Whole Planet," putting environmental sustainability at the core of its practices. Safeway's philosophy is to focus on providing "superior-quality products, a unique shopping experience, and customer-focused service" as stated on its website.

Examining some of its operational dimensions, we see that Whole Foods operates on a decentralized purchasing system, which empowers local product teams (i.e., fresh produce, seafood, and meat) to make departmental merchandising and pricing decisions for each store and support sourcing from local farmers as much as possible. Whole Foods sells healthy, organic, and gourmet groceries, but profits largely from its cooked food deli section. In contrast, traditional grocers such as Safeway assumes that it will profit from offering a broad range of merchandise (stock keeping units known as SKUs), competitive pricing, and maintaining locations in every major suburb. Most of its revenue comes from selling traditional food and drug items and a centralized purchasing system that does not emphasize local sourcing.

The innovative and successful business design pioneered by Whole Foods has created significant shareholder value and caused value to migrate away from traditional outdated business designs. For example, Safeway's 2012 revenue was close to $44 billion with a market capitalization of $7.6 billion and per employee sales of $44,400 annually (number of common stocks multiplied by its stock value as of September 25, 2013). By contrast, Whole Foods' 2012 revenue was $12.7 billion with a market capitalization of $12.85 billion and an annual per employee sale of $169,000. Whole Foods has managed to generate 1.7 times more shareholder value and employee sales of 3.8 times over Safeway, an indication that Whole Foods' business design is superior and more profitable than Safeway's.

BUSINESS DESIGN	WHOLE FOODS	SAFEWAY
Fundamental Assumption	Whole Foods: natural, organic, nutritious Whole People: treat people well Whole Planet: sustainable farming	Price, value, variety, accessibility
Customer Selection	Natural, health and sustainability conscious, "foodies," niche	Middle class, value conscious, mass market
Value Capture	Natural/organic and quality cooked food	Groceries drugs (pharmacy) and gasoline
Differentiation / Strategic Control	Sustainability, support of local farmers, group motivation	Product variety, accessible locations
Product Scope	Mainly organic, natural, local produce when possible	Full range
Go-to-market	Upper income, health and environmentally conscious	Low and middle income
Investment	Retail and merchandising, sustainability and green practices	Retail and merchandising
Organization	Decentralized, local group decision making and motivation	Traditional central command and control

The Case Illustrated

Let us now transfer the business design comparison between Whole Foods and Safeway onto a business design template designed by Adrian J. Slywotzky in his and David J. Morrison's book *The Profit Zone* (1999):

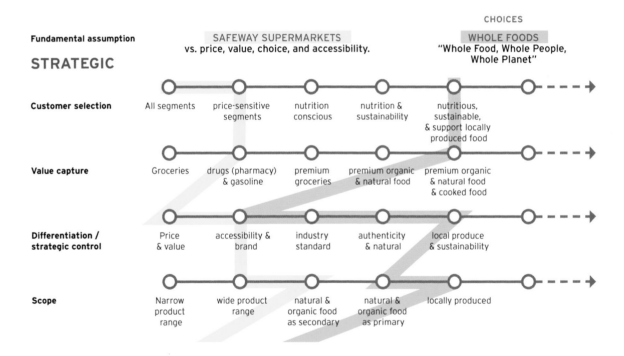

OPERATING

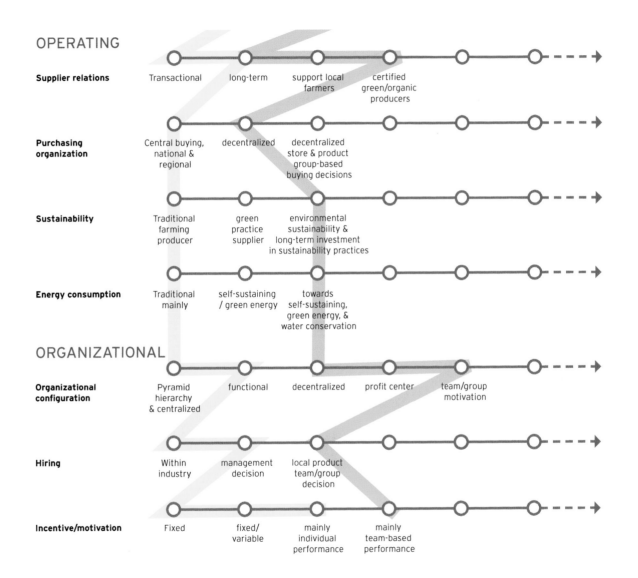

Supplier relations
Transactional — long-term — support local farmers — certified green/organic producers

Purchasing organization
Central buying, national & regional — decentralized — decentralized store & product group-based buying decisions

Sustainability
Traditional farming producer — green practice supplier — environmental sustainability & long-term investment in sustainability practices

Energy consumption
Traditional mainly — self-sustaining / green energy — towards self-sustaining, green energy, & water conservation

ORGANIZATIONAL

Organizational configuration
Pyramid hierarchy & centralized — functional — decentralized — profit center — team/group motivation

Hiring
Within industry — management decision — local product team/group decision

Incentive/motivation
Fixed — fixed/variable — mainly individual performance — mainly team-based performance

Preserve Key Continuities

While completing your new business design innovation exercise, always remember to be guided by your new bets and vision. Your business design is, in essence, your strategy formulation. The key is to understand which of those choices are best aligned to help you achieve your organization's fundamental assumption and mission and vision.

Once you have selected your strategic choices, you should link all of your choices by connecting the dots. A much different visual zig-zag appearance from the current design indicates that you have chosen a quite different set of strategies to compete with in the future.

Your strategic choices and elements for the new business design need not be entirely different from your current model, depending on your bets, business fundamental assumptions, and strategy. It can contain some current elements combined with newly invented ones. Change is not always about discarding current strategic choices in favor of new choices. In fact, change is often about preserving key continuities (such as brand, core competence, key customer relations) that will actually help drive the success of new elements.

DO IT YOURSELF

Here is a blank template for you to complete. In each platform, modify both the dimensions and strategic choices based on your industry. You can choose multiple strategic choices within a dimension as appropriate. Complete it for your own organization versus your competitors or for your current business design versus your future business redesign. Don't forget to link all of your choices by connecting the dots so you can see whether you have chosen a different set of strategies to compete with in the future and just how different they are.

Business Redesign: An Example Template

DIMENSIONS	CHOICES	OTHER CHOICES

Fundamental assumption

STRATEGIC

Customer selection

Value capture

Differentiation / strategic control

Scope

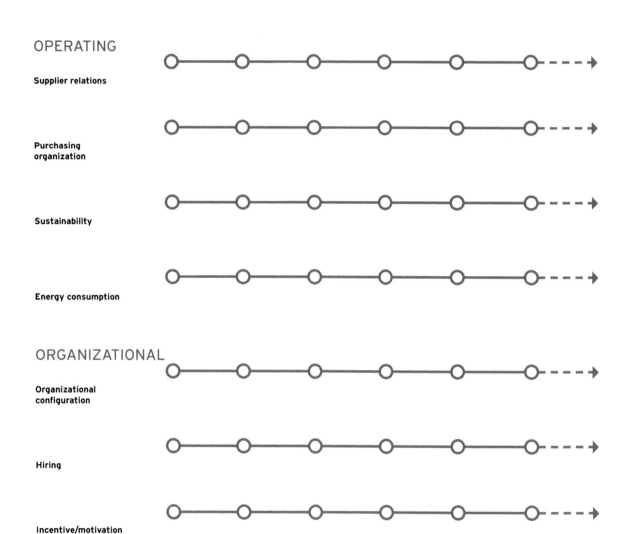

OPERATING

Supplier relations

Purchasing organization

Sustainability

Energy consumption

ORGANIZATIONAL

Organizational configuration

Hiring

Incentive/motivation

Source: From *The Profit Zone* by Adrian Slywotzky, David Morrison, and Bob Andelman, copyright © 1997. Used with permission of Random House.

Part 2

REDESIGN YOUR BUSINESS MODEL: THE FLOOR PLAN AND LAYOUT

You have completed the business design exercises and formulated the core strategy you will use to compete. However, now you need to operationalize this core strategy. How can you think through which tactics to use at an operational level? This is the key question you need to answer to develop your business model.

Continuing with the analogy of building a house, devising your new business design was like laying your structural foundation. For the next step, redesigning your business model is like deciding on the layout and floor plan of the house. The layout determines the location of your garage, living room, family room, den, kitchen and dining room, bedrooms, bathrooms, and other functional utility space. You can break down walls and connect these spaces in different ways, or remove this bathroom to make space for another bedroom, etc. The parallel in innovation is to prepare a business model to define your go-to-market competitive strategies and how all the components of your business will work together to help you achieve your business design. Specifically a business model can be defined as the rationale behind how an organization creates, delivers, and captures value.

Henry Chesbrough, a leading organizational theorist from the Haas School of Business, University of California, Berkeley, wrote a book, *Open Innovation* (2005), which describes how an organization creates, delivers,

and captures value in the form of a business model. There are nine key components that form the business model's outline and structure. These nine components are like the building blocks that show how a company intends to make money and organize itself. Alexander Osterwalder and Yves Pigneur in their innovative book *Business Model Generation* (2010) then used these nine key components to create a "business model canvas"– a simple template innovators and entrepreneurs can use to visualize their own business models.

To complete Part 2 of your master plan, in the following pages, we will:

A. Introduce the business model's nine building blocks.

B. Explain how the nine building blocks inter-relate to form a canvas.

C. Provide a summary of the canvas with examples.

D. Describe how to use the canvas for your own business model redesign.

E. Provide exercises to apply this knowledge.

Introducing the Nine Building Blocks of the Business Model

The book *Business Model Generation*, by Osterwalder and Pigneur, describes the nine building blocks or key components of the business model:

Customer Relationships: These are the types of relationships an organization establishes with its customer segments (e.g., personal vs. automated), which affect the customer experience.

Key Activities: These are the critical activities that need to be performed to make the business model work.

Value Proposition: These are the bundles of products or services that solve a problem or pain point for specific customers (i.e., create value).

Key Partnerships: These are the networks of suppliers and partners needed to make the business model work.

Customer Segments: These are the different groups of people or organizations an organization is trying to reach and serve.

Key Resources: These are critical assets needed to make the business model work.

Channels: These are the ways an organization communicates with and reaches its customer segments to deliver its value proposition.

Cost Structure: These are the costs incurred to operate the business model.

Revenue Streams: These are the ways cash is collected by the organization from the customer segments before or after delivering its value proposition successfully.

B   Introducing the Business Model Canvas

These nine building blocks of a business model inter-relate in important ways. Osterwalder and Pigneur used these nine key components to create a "business model canvas," which is a visual template and representation of the relationships between these building blocks. The template resembles a painter's canvas, which allows you to paint pictures of new or existing business models.

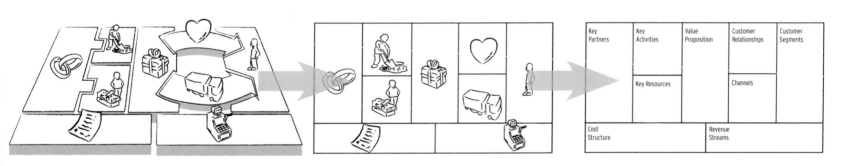

Source: *From Business Model Generation: a Handbook for Visionaries, Game Changers, and Challengers* by Alexander Osterwalder and Yves Pigneur. Reproduced with permission of Wiley in the format republish in a book via Copyright Clearance Center.

C The Business Model Canvas Simplified with Examples

Key Activities: What activities must you conduct to fulfill your promises to customers, support your distribution channels, and maintain superior customer relationships? (E.g., Google's key activities are its platform management, managing services, and expanding reach.)

Key Resources: What resources do you need to deliver your promise to customers? Key resources include intellectual property, human, financial, and physical assets. Not all key assets must be owned. Some can be acquired through strategic alliances with key partners or through outsourcing or leasing (e.g., key resources for American Express and other credit card companies are its credit/debit card transaction platform for customers, merchants, and banks. Google's search platform is a key asset in its business model).

Cost Structures: What are the fixed and variable cost structures inherent in your business model? How do you ensure your cost structure is lean and flexible with the lowest possible break-even point? A business model with low fixed costs (e.g., physical facilities, monthly rent, fixed salaries) and high variable costs (sales commissions, etc.) will have a lower break-even point (e.g., a mobile telecom company's main cost structure would be its network maintenance and marketing costs).

Key Partners: Who are your key suppliers in the value chain activity and what resources and value add are they providing? (E.g., Nespresso key partners are coffee machine manufacturers, high-end coffee growers, roasting plants, and high-end restaurants.)

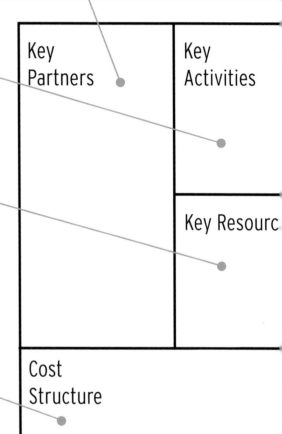

Value Propositions: What are the primary benefits that you are offering to your customers? (E.g., All automobile manufacturers create cars for transportation, but offer different value propositions. Volvo's value proposition is safety, BMW's is performance, Toyota's is reliability.)

Customer Relationship: What type of relationship do you want to establish with your target customers? (E.g., Dell uses the mass-customization model very successfully through its direct sales model, allowing customers to select modularized low-cost, mass-customized features.)

Customer Segments: Who are your target customer groups? Which groups do you want to serve and which segments do you want to ignore? (E.g., Whole Foods chooses to target higher income groups and natural and health food shoppers who support sustainable and eco-friendly practices and are less price sensitive than many other customers. They are not trying to appeal to the mass market, value-driven shoppers or bargain hunters.)

Channels: How do you reach your target customers and provide after sales support and service? (E.g., Amazon.com offers such support via the Internet without physical stores vs. Barnes and Noble relying mainly on its brick and mortar physical bookstores across the nation.)

Revenue Streams: How do you capture value through your product/service offerings? There are many ways to do this, such as sale of product/service for new and used goods, rental/leasing, subscription fees, usage fees, upgrades, licensing, etc. A business model with a one-time transaction revenue for product/service sales creates low value for business, whereas business models with recurring revenue streams, such as annuity payments, are more sustainable (e.g., mobile phone suppliers enjoy good revenue streams providing post-purchase value through long distance phone calls, text messaging service, and other upgraded internet video services and data plans).

Value Proposition

Customer Relationships

Customer Segments

Channels

Revenue Streams

D Using the Canvas for Business Model Redesign

The best way to show you how to use the canvas to develop your own business model redesign is to use an example. Using the example of the coffee industry, I will show you the successful business models of Starbucks and Nespresso to compare and contrast them. You can see how different choices in the various building blocks lead to very different business models. Both are successful in their own right, but compete in the same market in very different ways.

 NESPRESSO VERSUS STARBUCKS

Starbucks, based in Seattle, Washington, is the largest coffeehouse company in the world, with more than 20,000 coffee locations in more than 62 countries. The company sells coffee that it roasts along with other hot and cold beverages, pre-prepared food, and other coffee-related products. Starbucks has more than 149,000 employees, and had revenues of more than $13 billion in 2012. Their main value proposition is that coffee is an affordable luxury, and coffee drinking is an experience. This is in contrast to the coffee giants (Folgers, Maxwell House, etc.) of the 1980s who sold coffee as a commodity for the home and competed on the lowest prices in the grocery stores. Starbucks focuses on the coffee beans and roasting process to ensure that it offers a high-quality, good-tasting coffee. Moreover, its stores can customize your drink, with choices of coffee type (cappuccino, americano, etc.), type of milk, flavor shots, etc. Thus, the machines used are high-end and the company spends a great deal of time training staff to properly create the various types of drinks offered. Starbucks also sells high-end roasted beans, so you can enjoy the taste at home. In addition, its stores are comfortable and designed to serve as a social space to encourage customers to stay and enjoy the ambience.

Starbucks dominates very strategic locations in all major cities, holding long-term leases to fight for the position of being the "third place" customers spend the most time in, after the office and home. The company does not invest much in advertising.

Starbucks Business Model Canvas

Key Partners	Key Activities	Value Proposition	Customer Relationships	Customer Segments
Coffee growers; coffee roasters.	Production: coffee roasting; cafe operations; marketing but not much advertising.	Coffee is an affordable luxury; coffee is a culture and experience with ambience; one-to-one customization.	The third place (after work and home), social space for gathering.	Retail customers who visit their stores, grocery stores, specific airlines, specific restaurants.
	Key Resources Brand, coffee roasting plant.		**Channels** Company-owned Starbucks stores, Starbucks franchises, grocery stores and wholesale clubs, like Costco.	

Cost Structure	Revenue Streams
Coffee roasting, coffee shops rental, and barista staff.	Main revenue is from coffee sales, coffee beans, Starbucks grocery items sold in stores or by airlines.

Nespresso is the brand name of a gourmet espresso beverage system by Nestlé. Nespresso machines brew espresso from coffee capsules, which are pre-portioned single-use containers of ground coffee and flavorings. The capsules are used in a Nespresso coffee machine, designed to make high-quality, single-serving cups of espresso from the capsules at home or in small office settings. Packaged portions of espresso are a growing segment of the coffee market, accounting for an estimated 20% to 40% of the European coffee market, which totals $17 billion in sales. In the United States, Nestlé sells more than $1.9 billion worth of single-serve premium coffee for home consumption each year. Nespresso sales have been growing at an average rate of 30% to 35% per year over the past 10 years, and the company has sold more than 20 billion Nespresso capsules since 2000.

Nestlé holds patents for the service model, coffee machines, and espresso capsules (totaling 1,700 patents) to protect its market position. Nespresso capsules are sold exclusively through mail order via the company's own branded online Nespresso club, and it strongly advises against customers buying capsules from other sources. Its value proposition is that this product is an exclusive luxury for customers to enjoy at home, targeting high-income households that enjoy quality espresso. Nespresso invests heavily in marketing and advertising, using famous celebrities (e.g., actors George Clooney, John Malkovich, and Penelope Cruz) to advertise its product and brand. The company continues to focus solely on selling espresso and coffee in capsules, and has less than two dozen different flavor selections, deliberately choosing not to dilute the brand by selling other types of capsules, such as tea.

Nespresso Business Model Canvas

Key Partners	Key Activities	Value Proposition	Customer Relationships	Customer Segments
Coffee machine manufacturers.	Marketing; production; logistics.	High-end restaurant quality espresso at home; exclusive luxury item.	Nespresso club.	Households.
	Key Resources Distribution channels; patents on the coffee machine, service, and capsules; brand; production plants.		**Channels** Nespresso.com; Nespresso boutiques; call center; retail (machines only); mail order.	

Cost Structure	Revenue Streams
Manufacturing; marketing and advertising; distribution and channels	Main revenues: capsules; other: machines and accessories.

Source: From *Business Model Generation: a Handbook for Visionaries, Game Changers, and Challengers* by Alexander Osterwalder and Yves Pigneur. Reproduced with permission of Wiley in the format republish in a book via Copyright Clearance Center.

E Do It Yourself

Here's a blank canvas to help you think through your organization's business model:

1. Fill the business model canvas for your own innovation. Then do the same exercise for your key competitor(s) to visually identify what differentiates your strategy from theirs.

Your own innovation

Key Partners	Key Activities	Value Proposition	Customer Relationships	Customer Segments
	Key Resources		**Channels**	
Cost Structure			**Revenue Streams**	

Because it is visual, the canvas is particularly useful to work on in teams or to gain common understanding across a large team. Indeed, it is a hands-on tool that fosters understanding, discussion, creativity, and analysis. Groups of people in your organization can work together to sketch out and discuss elements of the canvas together by using Post-it® notes or white board markers to test out and discuss new redesign ideas.

Your key competitor

Key Partners	Key Activities	Value Proposition	Customer Relationships	Customer Segments
	Key Resources		Channels	

Cost Structure	Revenue Streams

2. Examine how your business model changes over time. First go back 10 to 20 years or more in your organization's history, and examine what the business model was like then and compare it to your current model. Then, project what you want your redesigned business model to look like 5 to 10 years from now. The purpose is to understand, in a historical context, how and why the organization has changed over time and to demonstrate that the organization has the capacity for change in many ways. Motivated readers can also do a business model canvas in the past, present, and future for their competitors as well. Of course, if you are a start-up, this may not be relevant.

FUTURE

PRESENT

PAST

Remember, the strategies you adopt in your business model need to be closely aligned with your shared View of the Future, and the business fundamental assumption and strategic choices of the elements in your business design. In total, your business model must closely address and help operationalize your future bets. For example, if your View of the Future envisions that more than 80% of all car sales in the next 10 to 15 years will be hybrid or electric cars, and your business fundamental assumptions are that people who want the convenience of transportation also care about the environment, then your business model choices, such as cost structure, must reflect a significant investment in perfecting the green technology and your key activities must relate closely to the research and development of new materials, parts, and components (batteries, charging stations, self-diagnostic device, etc.) to perfect the green car and show a significant reduction in research and innovation activities over those conducted on current fuel-driven models.

Part 3

CREATE A BUSINESS PLAN: THE CONSTRUCTION AND FINANCING PLAN

Once you have done the groundwork of devising a strong foundation and floor layout you must prepare an implementation plan. This involves creating a detailed timeline to delineate your cost breakdown, construction schedule, materials, labor costs, the permits required, and energy and environmental compliance standards. The equivalent in an innovation venture is preparing a business plan. At a high level, a business plan is a summary of your business's goals and how you plan to achieve them. This document should showcase the desirability, feasibility, and viability of your business idea, to communicate your idea to investors, partners, and other supporters from whom you will need to gain buy-in. You will need to define details such as the consumer pain points you are going to solve, potential market size and growth, your competition, operation and manufacturing plan, human resources, funding requirements, cash flow, return on investment projections, and the capital and equity structure of the venture. If you are introducing your innovation in the form of a start-up, you must also prepare a term sheet for your investors to delineate other detailed terms and conditions of the financing and operations plan.

To develop a good business plan, all the components need to be aligned seamlessly to support a unique value proposition in your business plan. The business plan must be realistic. In the case of venture capital (VC) funding, most VCs will water down 60% to 75% of the financial projection presented by most start-ups to adjust for risk and over-optimism.

Elements of the Business Plan

A good business plan is important because it describes who you are, your business, and shows how you will be profitable. It is essential for gaining investments from lenders and shareholders. I will not go in depth about how to write a good business plan as there are ample resources out there, but I want to summarize the main elements briefly for you, based on Jeffry Timmons and Stephen Spinelli's book, *New Venture Creation* (2008). In this book, they lay out the process and key questions to ask and answer when constructing a business plan.

Business Plan Master Checklist

1. **Executive summary:**
    - Description of business concept and the business (solving the pain points)
    - Target market and projections (size of market in $ and units)
    - Competitive advantage: Product/market positioning business model, value capture strategy
    - Costs
    - Return of investment, investor pay back, and sustainability
    - The team and the offering

2. **The industry, the company and its products/services:**
    - The industry
    - The company and the concept
    - The product(s)/service(s)
    - Entry and growth strategy

3. **Market research and analysis:**
    - Customers
    - Market size and trends
    - Competition and competitive edges
    - Estimated market share and sales
    - Ongoing market evaluation

4. The economics of the business:

- Business model: How do you organize delivery of products/ services? What is your revenue model? How do you monetize your service? What is your value capture strategy?

- Gross and operating margins

- Profit potential and durability

- Fixed, variable, and semi-variable costs

- Months to break even

- Months to reach positive cash flow

---

5. Marketing plan:

- Marketing mix strategy: Product/market positioning strategy

- Product/pricing/place/promotion

- Product roll out and launch campaign

- Pricing

- Sales tactics

- Services and warranty policies

- Branding: Brand experience and value proposition

- Distribution: Viral marketing

---

6. Technology, design, development plan:

- Development status and tacks

- Difficulties and risks

- Technology, product improvement, and new products

- Costs

- Proprietary issues (intellectual property rights and protection)

---

7. Manufacturing and operation plan:

- Operating cycle

- Geographical location

- Facilities and upgrades

- Strategy and plans

- Regulatory and legal issues

---

8. Management team:

- Organization
- Key management personnel
- Management compensation and ownership
- Other investors
- Employment and other agreements
- Stock option and bonus plan
- Board of directors, other shareholders, rights and restrictions
- Supporting professional advisors and services

9. Overall schedule:

- Overall timeline, schedule/milestones

10. Critical risks, problems, and assumptions:

- Product/technology risks, market risk, people risk, fatal flaw

11. The financial plan:

- Actual income statement and business balance sheet
- Pro forma income statements
- Pro forma balance sheet
- Pro forma cash flow analysis
- Break-even chart and calculation
- Cost control
- Highlights

12. Proposed company offering:

- Desired financing
- Offering
- Capitalization
- Use of funds
- Investors' return

13. Term sheet:

- Terms and conditions of acceptance of funding from investors

ADDRESSING REAL-WORLD TENSIONS THROUGH THE TAO

Chapter 6 so far is about formulating your complete business strategy, and how to think about your business design, your business model, and your business plan in tandem. The process of building this master plan is a way of structuring your fundamental set of assumptions or hypotheses and your accompanying go-to-market strategy. However, it is said that a business plan becomes obsolete once it is written. Once an innovation hits the market and is exposed to real customers, unpredictable conditions and unexpected factors always come into play. Major changes to your master plan are almost always required, but they can either be viewed as disturbances that cause the plan to veer off course or as opportunities to pause, reevaluate, and adjust.

As you answer this chapter's innovation question, "How do you design a strong and lasting go-to-market strategy?," be prepared to face tension between the values of:

PLANNED STRATEGY   VS.   EMERGENT STRATEGY

Your planned strategy is what you have carefully considered as the best way to position and differentiate your offerings from those of your competition to succeed in the market, often using the best-case scenario.

However, your emergent strategy is the process of making errors, then corrections and rapid iterations and adaptation based on changing market conditions and customer feedback on your new product offerings. This process of quickly adjusting and responding to the market and customers can lead to deviations and contradictions to your planned strategy, which can then cause the need to decide whether to stick to your planned strategy or switch in response to the emergent strategy and conditions.

To reconcile the tension between following your plan and adapting to the unexpected, you need to:

Continuously craft the emergent strategy to improve the effectiveness of the planned strategy.

Emergent Strategy

Planned Strategy

The reconciliation between planned strategy and emergent strategy is to see strategy formulation and implementation as an iterative exercise in which you are continuously crafting the emergent strategy to improve the effectiveness of the planned strategy. Innovators need to realize that failure is an integral part of fine-tuning your strategy and searching for a more sustainable business model for your new business. You are looking to "fail forward" along the iteration journey to avoid making the same mistakes twice. You want to return to the market swiftly with corrections that better meet the real needs and expectations of your customers.

Strategy should not be executed rigidly or blindly, or fail to reflect the latest market conditions and customer feedback. Instead strategy should be seen as a crafting process through which you continuously fine-tune your planned strategy to account for emerging conditions.

[*Case in Point*] HONDA SUPER CUB

A classic case of how a planned strategy was successfully adjusted into an emergent strategy is how Honda stumbled its way into the US motorbike market in the late 1950s with its Super Cub 50 cc small motorbikes. The Super Cub was inspired by the popularity of small mopeds and lightweight motorcycles used in Europe, but at the outset seemed to have no market potential in the United States where most popular motorbikes were much more powerful, in the 250–350 cc category. Honda's original plan was to sell large motorbikes at a significantly lower cost to compete in the US market against brands like Harley-Davidson and Triumph. Only a very low volume of Super Cubs were imported, meant to be used by Honda employees for running errands around town. To Honda's dismay, early on their large motorbikes had serious performance and mechanical issues on the road and were viewed as inferior, cheap versions of their competitors' models.

While the engineers in Japan were trying to redesign the engines to catch up with their competitors in the large motorbike category, Honda's staff was riding the 50 cc Super Cub around the Los Angeles area to run errands and for fun. They began to attract a lot of attention from locals, including a buyer at Sears who wanted to offer the mini-motorbike to Sears' customers. While Honda had assumed the small bike was unsuitable for the US market, its original strategy to compete in the 250–350 cc category was plagued with many problems. The company somewhat reluctantly agreed to import more Super Cubs into the United States and worked with an advertising agency to position the bike as a lifestyle product for younger buyers who were looking for something light and inexpensive for short trips around metro areas, in stark contrast to the stereotypical "black leather bikers" and more hard-core brands such as Harley-Davidson.

The Super Cub 50 cc became a big hit and Honda embraced its emergent strategy to focus on dominating the small bike category. Over the next few decades, Honda improved the Super Cub's features and power in subsequent models, and also expanded the sales successfully to Europe and Asia. It now stands as the highest-produced and best-selling motor vehicle in the world. Honda's fate in the motorcycle market would have been drastically different had it insisted on sticking to its planned strategy and original assumptions.

How do you craft a strong and lasting go-to-market strategy?

Answering this question starts with the practice of:

Building the Master Plan

▼ Rethink the fundamental assumption of your business and craft an innovative business redesign using the templates provided. Invent and create new strategic options, incorporating your new bets under each of the dimensions appropriate to your business. These strategic options form your business design and visually demonstrate how you are attempting to shape the industry going forward with solid strategic control points. While you want to differentiate yourself based on solid strategic control points, you also need to ensure that certain dimensions are continued and preserved in order to facilitate change.

▼ Create and invent a new business model using the templates provided. This model will reflect the change in elements and activities such as types of supplier networks, core activities, new value propositions, new customer types, new channels of distribution, new revenue streams, and new cost structures. Again, be sure the new business model is driven by the new bets you laid from the View of the Future and closely aligns with the strategic imperatives laid out by the business design.

▼ Develop a complete and integrated business plan using the template provided to prepare yourself for funding requirements.

Want to go deeper?

Further Reading

Blank, S. and Dorf, B. (2012). *The startup owner's manual*. Pescadero, CA: K&S Ranch, Inc.

Chesbrough, H. (2006). *Open business models*. Boston, MA: Harvard Business School Press.

Osterwalder, A., Pigneur, Y. and Clark, T. (2010). *Business model generation*. Hoboken, NJ: Wiley.

Ries, E. (2011). *The lean startup*. New York, NY: Crown Business.

Slywotzky, A. (1996). *Value migration*. Boston, MA: Harvard Business School Press.

Slywotzky, A., Morrison, D. and Andelman, B. (1997). *The profit zone*. New York, NY: Times Business.

Timmons, J. and Spinelli, S. (2008). *New venture creation: Entrepreneurship for the 21st century* (8th ed.). United Kingdom: Irwin Professional Pub.

How do you know if your idea can survive in the real world?

Thunder symbolizes "the way" to answer this question.

Thunder SHAKES, anticipating a storm to come

It represents the practice of Passing the Stress Test.

How do you know whether your idea can survive in the real world?

WHY IS THIS QUESTION IMPORTANT?

A great deal of ingenuity and thinking has gone into your business idea, but what will actually happen when you enter the market is unpredictable. While there are no guarantees, there are ways to make your business plan more foolproof and test how well your plan can withstand consumer, competitive, and market forces.

*A*fter you have developed your business master plan (covered in Chapter 6) it is time to take a step back to assess whether your strategy and plan are strong enough to survive when the ground shakes from the thunder of market forces. There are major go-to-market issues that need to be considered before implementation so that you can anticipate and address the range of real-world challenges you are likely to confront. This chapter presents a holistic stress test that evaluates your plan against most fundamental business issues, which can also predict how well you will thrive in the market. Furthermore, if you need to raise external funding, support, or buy-in, any experienced investor, partner, or stakeholder will be concerned about these same issues. Up until now, many of your efforts have been focused on developing, defining, and planning. Now it is time for a reality check.

STEPS FOR YOUR ACTION PLAN	WHAT THEY HELP YOU ACCOMPLISH
Business Definition Test	Assess whether your existing business scope and definition can support and fit your innovation
Triple Lens Test	Assess whether your product can be implemented in the real world through the lenses of desirability, feasibility, and viability

BUSINESS DEFINITION TEST

If you are innovating within an existing firm or corporate environment (as opposed to a start-up), the innovation and new business you are proposing needs to fit into your organization's existing general business definition or you will have trouble securing high-level, long-term commitment and resources. In former Harvard professor Derek F. Abell's hallmark book, *Defining the Business* (1980), he pioneered the concept of a "Three-Dimensional Business Definition model," stressing the need for corporations to define their business in a broader sense, driven by a consumer-oriented perspective rather than a narrow product or capabilities-oriented manner. For example, rather than saying, "We are in the railway business," a railway company should broaden its business definition by saying, "We are in the transportation business." IBM strategically defines its business as being in the information processing and storage business rather than simply saying that it manufactures computers or storage devices. Start-ups should also think broadly about their business definitions to accommodate potential major shifts in customer needs in the future.

Test your master plan by asking, "Is my existing business definition broad enough to encompass my new innovation?"

If not, it is time to rethink what you are "in the business of"—or your innovation may not be a good fit for your organization.

This may seem like a simple test but is critical to the fundamental progress of your innovation.

TRIPLE LENS STRESS TEST

The Triple Lens Test is a high-level, yet holistic way to evaluate the strength and potential of an innovation. It focuses on three key "lenses" of desirability, feasibility, and viability, inspired by IDEO's human-centered design thinking process (also referenced in Chapter 4 about inspiring breakthrough ideas). These three lenses are all critical drivers of innovation and any successful idea, project, or venture needs to sit at the overlap of all three.

These three lenses provide a simple framework to categorize more specific go-to-market issues that you must consider and for which you must plan. Not all issues may be relevant to your innovation, but collectively they prepare you for tough questions and help you think through strategic requirements.

Below is a high-level, quick, and easy tool that you can use to evaluate your innovation. It is an integration of the three lenses of innovation and key elements taken from the industry's go-to tool for assessing business opportunities called the Quick Screen Test, by Jeffry A. Timmons and Stephen Spinneli, in their book *New Venture Creation: Entrepreneurship for the 21st Century*.

You will see that there are a great deal of technical business and financing terms used in this tool. If any of the terms below are unfamiliar to you, it's a good time to read up on them. Any potential investors will be expecting you to understand them.

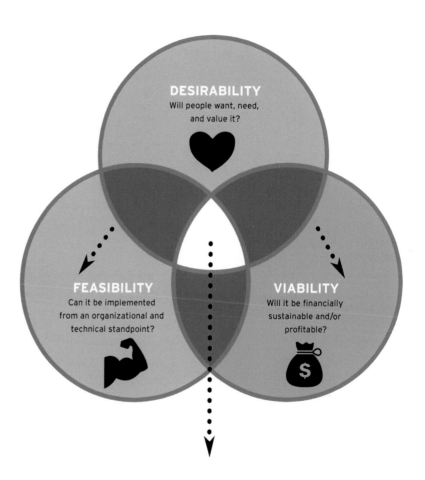

DESIRABILITY
Will people want, need, and value it?

FEASIBILITY
Can it be implemented from an organizational and technical standpoint?

VIABILITY
Will it be financially sustainable and/or profitable?

ASSESSMENT CRITERIA FOR DESIRABILITY	LOW ATTRACTIVENESS	HIGH ATTRACTIVENESS
1. Idea/Solution Attractiveness		
a. Significance of pain point/problem/ needs and wants addressed by innovation	Solves trivial problems	Sovles significant obstacle or bottlenecks
b. Degree that innovation can solve pain point over current solutions	Incremental difference	Dramatic difference
c. Payback time to users, length of time to recover cost of investment or receive full benefit	> 3 years	< 1 year
2. Market Attractiveness		
a. Market size	< $10 million or > $1 billion	$50-100 million in first 5-7 years is a typical benchmark for VCs
b. Market growth rate potential (annual)	< 20%, a declining product category	> 20%, likely to become a major product category

Going Deeper into Desirability

- Is the market for your innovation well defined or will you be responsible for defining it?

- How strong and focused is your value proposition (to the consumer/user)?

- How reachable and receptive are your target customers? How loyal are they to existing brands/offerings?

- How user friendly is your product, service, and/or overall user experience?

Source: Adapted from New Venture Creation: Entrepreneurship for the 21st Century by Jeffry Timmons and Stephen Spinelli, copyright © 2008. Reproduced with permission by McGraw-Hill Education.

ASSESSMENT CRITERIA FOR FEASIBILITY	LOW ATTRACTIVENESS	HIGH ATTRACTIVENESS
1. Product/Technology Development Capability		
a. Technology hurdle faced by organization (e.g., R&D, accessibility, cost and reliability of technology required)	High technical hurdle	Low technical hurdle
b. Product development hurdle faced by organization (e.g., design, approval standards, quality, cost management, speed)	Cost ineffectiveness	Competitive and able to acquire approval standards
2. Degree/Extent of Competitive Advantage		
a. IP and proprietary/contractual advantage	Weak, none	Secure, exclusive
b. Resource and capability generation time advantage (product, tech, team, location, time to market)	No edge	Strong edge, slow competition
3. Network and Supply Chain Relationship Advantage	None, limited	Strong, exclusive
4. Distribution Channel Advantage	None, limited	Strong, exclusive

Product development and manufacturing:

- Will the technology/product work according to its performance specifications, like the prototype?

  _____

- Will it survive a "life test" according to the design criteria (e.g., testing whether a LED light bulb fulfills its promise of a 50,000-hour life)? Will it pass all the required standards of approval (e.g., FDA approval for food and drugs, UL certification for electronics), patent right, or licensing agreement acquisition?

  _____

- Can it be manufactured on a large-scale basis?

  _____

- Can manufacturing either in-house, outsourcing, or a combination of both be organized on a timely basis to support launch?

  _____

- Will it be ready within the product development timeline?

  _____

- Is there any fatal flaw that would kill the project before launch (e.g., failure to acquire FDA approval for a new drug)?

  _____

Team:

- Do you have a strong team of high energy and passionate people who have a strong sense of purpose and desire to succeed?

  _____

- Does the team have talent with diverse backgrounds?

  _____

- Do members have deep domain knowledge of the field? Are they technically and operationally competent to see the new product launch through and beyond?

  _____

- Is there strong leadership in the team?

  _____

- Is the team adaptive in execution and able to cope with changing circumstances and unpredictability in the early start-up stage?

  _____

- Does the team have access to advisors and mentors with broad networking capabilities to help in the initial stage of the launch?

  _____

- For all the above questions regarding the team, what are your gaps, and who do you need to add or remove to strengthen your team?

  _____

Going Deeper into Feasibility

- Do you have the resources and capabilities to implement your new innovation?

- Does your organizational structure allow you to deliver and move quickly enough to respond to changing market needs? If not, are you positioned to acquire them externally or grow them internally?

ASSESSMENT CRITERIA FOR VIABILITY	LOW ATTRACTIVENESS	HIGH ATTRACTIVENESS
1. Gross Margin and Cost Structure		
a. Gross margin %	< 20% and fragile	> 40-50% for durable goods, 50-60% for services, and 60-75% for software/web-based products or services is ideal
b. Fixed and variable costs and burn-rate (monthly start-up expenses)	Highest	Low fixed cost, high variable cost and monthly burn-rate
2. Profit and Payback		
a. Gross profit margin		
b. Market size	< $10 million or + $1 billion	$50-100 million in the first 5-7 years is a typical benchmark for VCs
c. Profit after tax	< 5%, fragile	10-15% more and durable
d. Time to break even	> 3 years	< 2 years
e. Time to positive cash flow	> 3 years	< 2 years
f. ROI potential	< 20%, fragile	40-70% more, durable, 25% or more is considered high potential venture
g. Capital requirements	Very high; difficult to fund	Low to moderate; fundable
h. Exit mechanism	Undefined, illiquid investment	Trade Sale, Initial Public Offering (IPO) or Merger and Acquisition (M&A)

Going Deeper into Viability

- What is the venture's free cash-flow stream?
  Twenty to thirty percent of sales or more is favorable.

- What is the projected sales/revenue growth?
  Twenty to thirty percent is ideal.

- Can the market support a pricing level for an
  adequate gross margin of 50% and upward in the
  initial stage of product introduction and rapid product
  adoption stage?

NEW INNOVATIONS AND EXISTING BUSINESSES REQUIRE DIFFERENT BENCHMARKS

To help ascertain whether the innovation/venture idea and plan has a high likelihood of success, I encourage innovators to assess their projects and business plans against these criteria before asking for funding. In the case of innovation within an existing firm, I recommend that firms not use their established mainstream core business financial threshold to assess a new product/venture opportunity or the entire project will have a short life without adequate funding and resource support.

Emphasis must be placed on the long term; specifically consideration of the impact the new product can have on existing business and customers over time. Companies that succeed in introducing disruptive innovation often incubate new ideas outside and separately from their core businesses, providing a highly entrepreneurial environment for the start-up team with different key performance indicators that allow necessary time for growth.

DID YOU PASS OR FAIL?

These tests are not meant to definitively determine whether your master plan and strategy are good or bad. They are meant to give you a general sense of how fit or healthy your strategy is and where it might have weaknesses or oversights that you need to address. If you passed most of the tests (scoring "high attractiveness" for most criteria), congratulations! Your chances of success are good and you should feel confident enough to proceed with your plan. If you failed on a few criteria here or there, don't be discouraged. You should further investigate which aspects are critical to the success of your idea and which ones are not relevant or essential to your situation. If there are critical gaps, think about the best way to go about filling them. However, if you failed on most of them, you should be worried. This is a red flag indicating trouble ahead if you do not revisit the drawing board to work out the key issues.

In this chapter so far, I have provided you with tools to test the overall fitness level of your innovation master plan so that you can self-assess your venture's attractiveness before presenting it to secure internal or external support and funding. It is normal for this process to reveal gaps or overlooked areas that you will need to go back and address. As you take a step back to evaluate your strategies and plans from a big picture viewpoint, it can be hard to be objective and open to criticism. Know that innovator(s) or founding team members tend to overestimate early product adoption rates and underestimate the expenses and investment (burn rate) involved to fund the project.

As you answer this chapter's innovation question, "How do you know whether your idea can survive in the real world?," be prepared to face tension between the values of:

OPTIMISM VS. CONSERVATISM

Optimism can be a double-edged sword. Innovators must be optimistic to survive. This positive attitude and sense of conviction is the core to believing in your vision, rallying support, and having the fortitude to move beyond obstacles and skeptics. In the interest of attracting investments and supporters, it is only natural to present an optimistic, best-case scenario market and financial projections. Investors know this and it is not uncommon for them to discount as much as 75% of the financial projections in business plan proposals with "hockey stick-like" earning streams and cash flow projections, which show a sudden sharp upswing.

On the other extreme, some innovators may be overly conservative in building projections, for fear of over-promising and under-delivering. Conservative projections limit risk exposure and can thus be seen as more realistic and honest.

To reconcile the tension between being optimistic and conservative, you need to:

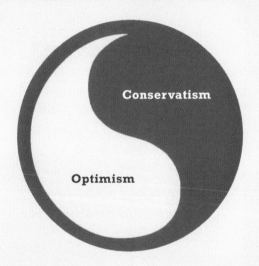

Validate your master plan through rounds of iteration and refinement to generate market and customer tested data as the basis for more realistic financial projections.

Innovators need to have the patience and discipline to test the assumptions and hypotheses they make about their business models by getting user feedback, prototyping, and learning from variations of fundamental ideas, and iterating and refining ideas to come up with data points and projections that are as realistic as possible. If you have gone through this process, potential investors are more likely to believe your financial data because they are informed by early consumer and market insights.

In short, your assumptions and the building blocks of your business plans must be realistic. This will help potential investors to more accurately consider the financial attractiveness and the risk-reward profile of your innovation, and how it compares with similar ventures funded most recently in your industry.

THUNDER 雷

How do you know whether your idea can survive in the real world?

Answering this question starts with the practice of:

Passing the Stress Test

▼ Assess your idea against the business definition test to see whether it aligns with your current organization.

▼ Identify which criteria in the Triple Lens Test are relevant to your innovation.

▼ Use the Triple Lens Test to help you assess whether a key stakeholder or investor would consider your innovation attractive and strong enough to support or fund.

Want to go deeper?

Further Reading

Timmons, J. A. and Spinelli, S. (2008). *New venture creation: Entrepreneurship for the 21st century*. Boston, MA: McGraw-Hill/Irwin.

Abell, D. F. (1980). *Defining the business: The starting point of strategic planning*. Englewood Cliffs, NJ: Prentice-Hall.

How do you scale successfully?

Wind symbolizes the "the way"
to answer this question.

Wind SPREADS. It is the power of
diffusion. This element inspires us
to continue to grow and expand in
an effective and efficient way.

Wind represents the practice of
Preparing for Rapid Growth.

How do you scale successfully?

WHY IS THIS QUESTION IMPORTANT?

Most ventures fail during the scaling process; yet the ability to scale is key to growing a profitable and sustainable business. The skills that helped to establish and launch an innovation are not the same type of expertise required for scaling and taking a start-up to the next level. To succeed in the long term, many informal or improvised ways of working need to transition into the right attitude, people, and processes in place to avoid execution pitfalls.

*M*ore than 600,000 new ventures are launched each year in America, but fewer than 20% survive for more than two years. Of those that survive, fewer than 10% are able to scale into a sizable business with more than 100 employees within five years, and go on to become a growing and viable venture. Part of the challenge is the massive changes that occur in an organization when you scale. Here, I provide some tips for ventures to continue their growth path and manage some of the challenges and changes that are likely to occur. These tips will help you get to the next stage of sustainable enterprise.

STEPS FOR YOUR ACTION PLAN	WHAT THEY HELP YOU ACCOMPLISH
Follow the early adopters	Learn from your early customers to understand key motivations and drivers
Use customer acquisition and conversion metrics	Use market data to focus on customer acquisition, engagement, and retention
Iterate and allow for rapid errors and corrections	Have a rapid feedback loop to allow you to make quick improvements
Sharpen your "killer application"	Focus on propagating your key value proposition
Secure key reference accounts	Leverage reputable and influential customers early on to convince others to take the plunge
Standardize operational procedures	Put rule-based systems, process, structures, and policies in place
Do not diversify too early	Do not diversify your efforts until you have achieved market traction and tested your business model hypotheses
Be conscious of shifts in your culture	Design a culture that can sustain change and growth as you scale
Stay focused and committed	Maintain stakeholder confidence and support

THE STAGES OF ENTREPRENEURIAL TRANSITION

To describe the different stages and challenges that ventures tend to go through as they scale to become established businesses, we reference a pioneer in the study of entrepreneurship and education research Jeffry Timmons, who co-wrote the leading entrepreneurial textbook with Stephen Spinelli, *New Venture Creation* (2009). In this book they suggest an entrepreneurial transition model, composed of four stages: planning, doing and execution, leading, and leading managers. You can use this as a quick and easy reference to think about where your venture currently is and what organizational changes you may face ahead.

STAGE 2

||||||||||||||||||||||||||||||||||||||||||||||||||||||||||||||||||||||||||||||||||||||||||||||||||||||||||||||

STAGE 1

||||||||||||||||||||||||||||||||||||||||||||||||||||||||||||||||||||||||||||||||||||||||||||||||||||

According to Timmons, in **stage 1** of the venture creation process, the team typically grows from zero to five. At this stage there may be no sales or profit at all. Change is wrenching and resources are limited. Planning is the main task at this nascent stage.

In **stage 2**, when the team grows to 20 to 30 people, sales can be $0-5 million. Uncertainty, ambiguity, and inexperience begin to show and change is constant. The focus is on doing and execution.

STAGE 3

|||||||||||||||||||||||||||||||||||||||||||||||||||||||||||||||||||||||||||||

In stage 3, when the team grows to 25 to 75 people, sales can reach $10-15 million. Creativity can slow down, roles and responsibilities can be unclear, and the desire for autonomy and to delegate rather than control is strong. The focus is now on leading the team and organization and strategy, operating systems, process, structure, and policies become vitally important.

STAGE 4

|||||||||||||||||||||||||||||||||||||||||||||||||||||||||||||||||||||||||||||||||||||||||||||||||||

Finally, in stage 4, when the team expands beyond 75 to 100 people with sales of typically $10 million or more, collaboration can erode due to increased complexity. The practice of influence management and the execution of power and conflict resolution become obvious in the organization. The need for strong operating controls cannot be underestimated. At this point, the entrepreneurial transition switches from leading to leading managers.

FOLLOW THE EARLY ADOPTERS

Scaling a venture is about accelerating the product adoption rate and implementing your fine-tuned business model.

Everett Rogers, who coined the popular term "early adopters" in his book *Diffusion of Innovation* (1962), theorized that innovation is spread along the innovation adoption curve. The rate of adoption is the relative speed at which consumers or members of a social system adopt an innovation. Most innovations start off with new product adoption rates as follows: innovators (2.5%), then early adopters (13.5%), early majority (34%), late majority (34%), and laggards (16%). With the rate of diffusion adoption eventually reaches critical mass, at which point the adoption becomes self-sustaining and continues to grow.

New ventures begin with the design phase, launch, scaling, and then diversification. After you have designed and launched your new innovation, you must stay very close to your early customers (the 2.5% early adopters of new products) and learn about their key motivations for switching to your new product. Setting your venture up for success by fine-tuning your product positioning strategy and developing an enthusiastic sales distribution channel network are the most important drivers of scaling your venture at the early stage. Understanding what motivates consumers to purchase and use your products is critical in getting their support for your rapid growth and insight into how to best refine your offering.

Many innovators get stuck in the chasm between early adopters and early majority. The rest of this chapter presents some in-field advice which can help increase your chances of scaling faster and reaching the late majority.

While the innovation adoption curve is relevant to many businesses, as explained in Chapter 3, Larry Downes and Paul F. Nunes argued in their book *Big Bang Disruption* that more and more disruptive innovations today (especially Internet-based applications or products) do not follow normal patterns of market adoption.

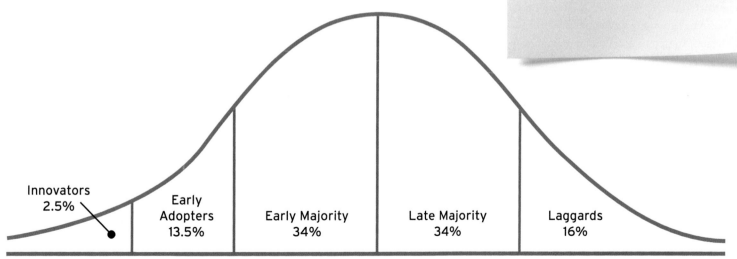

Innovators
2.5%

Early Adopters
13.5%

Early Majority
34%

Late Majority
34%

Laggards
16%

USE CUSTOMER ACQUISITION AND CONVERSION METRICS

When you reach the point at which you are satisfied with your business model and margin structure and are getting a good early adoption rate, you are faced with the question of where to scale next. Just because a product or service is successful in one location does not mean that it will also be successful in another geography or market. Developing meaningful customer acquisition and conversion metrics becomes critical before you spread your product distribution to a new location, across the country or globally.

 AMAZONFRESH

Amazon.com is determined to enter the online home delivery grocery business because of its enormous market potential, through the company AmazonFresh. The total US food retail market is estimated to be worth around $500 billion, and if you add specialized and other diverse channels this moves up to $1 trillion. Within that, the online grocery market was estimated to be worth $15.4 billion in 2013 by Forrester Research, a global research and advisory firm.

Amazon is utilizing its customer acquisition and route efficiency metrics data to validate its business model. The company's customer acquisition data are leading them to expand only into high-density urban neighborhoods with the demographics that meet their customers' acquisition matrices. Understanding customer demographics at the neighborhood level is a critical factor of success. AmazonFresh had been tested for years in selected neighborhoods in Seattle, Washington, where Amazon is headquartered. To date, its program still does not cover the entire Seattle area. It expanded very carefully in July 2013 to target high-density urban locations in Los Angeles and to some San Francisco Bay Area neighborhoods. It has plans to scale to as many as 20 other markets in 2014 and beyond.

AmazonFresh is betting on its massive existing user base, iCloud IT infrastructure, cross-selling of other merchandise, and its highly efficient automated warehouse workforce to make the online groceries business successful at scale. The company is using these Amazon platforms to understand customer preferences and behaviors. If AmazonFresh succeeds in scaling in a big way, it will change the way we shop for groceries—completely online—in the future.

Dropbox is a highly successful online backup (file synchronization) and data storage firm with more than 200 million users in 2013. Dropbox's founder, Drew Houston, realized early on that Dropbox needed to ensure that the marketing messages and pricing structure were optimized. Thus, Houston dedicated as much as 30% of his engineering resources at the early growth stage to hire an analytics engineer (his eighth employee), whose job was to focus on tracking metrics that helped the company understand patterns in user behaviors along the chain of activities from sign-up, usage, to eventual purchase, to optimize customer acquisition and engagement efforts. Some of the key metrics included:

- acquisition of landing page visitors;

- activation of these visitors into users;

- retention of users;

- referral of new visitors by satisfied users; and

- revenue earned from users.

When deciding whether to offer a single product for both consumer and business users, they tracked users by weighing two factors: whether they shared files with others and whether they used the application for business. Their early consumer metrics led to the creation of a single product for its mass users and business enterprise customers. Based on their data, they have employed a "freemium" strategy (the first gigabyte of storage is free and a small monthly fee is charged for additional storage space) to drive customer product adoption. For business users, they offer a slightly higher monthly fee for much more storage space.

ITERATE AND ALLOW FOR RAPID ERRORS AND CORRECTIONS

Once you start implementing your new business model strategy, you will begin the process of experimentation. Innovation and experimentation is a continuous process with many rounds of iterations. It is critical to have a rapid and continuous user feedback system to help fine-tune any kinks in your experimentation model during this early learning curve. This helps you to correct your errors and keep up the momentum along the diffusion curve, continuing to grow your user base.

The design and innovation process is an ever-changing evolution. Therefore, innovators do not have to wait until the product is 100% perfect before launching it. Instead, innovators launch their best prototypes, knowing that there will be updated versions on the horizon based on user feedback. The goal for innovators is to avoid making the same mistakes twice and try to get it right in the shortest possible amount of time.

Examples abound of the need for iteration *while* you innovate. Edison's electric light bulb and the Dyson vacuum cleaner both went through over a thousand iterations and continuous improvements. Apple Computer launched its first model of the iPad with minimum product features and very quickly came back the second year to introduce the iPad 2 with product improvements guided by customer feedback on the mistakes in the first model. The iPad is now in its fifth generation and each one incorporates new features, continuous innovation, and incremental improvements. Many other business models employ rapid iterations, such as cellular phones, cars, computer software—all of which have updated versions coming to market over the span of several years. Testing your business model hypotheses is critical before scaling takes place. The iterative process of making rapid errors and corrections to improve the product is critical in the scaling stage, since your innovation is probably a product or service that has never been manufactured, sold, or used much before in the exact same way you intend. Each subsequent version should be better than the previous one. The result is continuous cycles of improvement and change.

SHARPEN YOUR "KILLER APPLICATION"

Scaling requires you to focus on propagating a unique "killer application," a feature or offering that addresses a need or want so well that it becomes the key draw for purchasing the larger product or system. When personal computers first entered the market, word processing and spreadsheets were the killer apps that drove many people to purchase their first computers. Email and search engines were the killer apps of the Internet boom in the 1990s. As mentioned earlier, you must also design a system to receive fast feedback on how to fine-tune your product offerings quickly and to make sure your product performs well for early adopters. Most importantly it has to have a strong killer application that is designed to solve significant customers pain points and become the "must have" product or service of your industry.

SECURE KEY REFERENCE ACCOUNTS

A reference account refers to when reputable customers use your product or service. Securing a key reference account is very helpful as a testimony from credible early adopters and to convince other enthusiastic consumers to join the crowd of early adopters. It is a very low-cost and effective way to scale your revenue at the early stage. Some entrepreneurs offer free samples to key reference accounts to entice other customers to join in.

STANDARDIZE OPERATIONAL PROCEDURES

Once your venture's initial launch is successful, you will experience a rapid increase in revenue and adoption rate. The team must have talent with operational background to focus on the execution of orders and begin to put rule-based systems, processes, structures, and policies in place to standardize operational procedures and ensure smooth execution and implementation of plans. You must however remain nimble, flexible, and able to change to meet and exceed customers' needs.

DO NOT DIVERSIFY TOO EARLY

Do not diversify your efforts until you have achieved market traction with minimum scale and growth momentum. Build and stabilize your team, finances, brand, and star product before you look at diversification. If you diversify too early, you will dilute your message to your customer and change your positioning before you have fully secured it. Once you have earned credibility in an area of specialization, you will have more leverage as you enter new areas.

BE CONSCIOUS OF SHIFTS IN YOUR CULTURE

Founders of start-ups want to build entrepreneurial teams to jumpstart their ventures. When you decide to grow, it is just as critical to build a sustainable culture to increase your organizational capacity to scale the enterprise. The challenge is balancing and retaining characteristics of both a start-up and the larger, more structured organization that you want to become or are becoming. How do you blend the best of both worlds and make the necessary transitions?

Building a multi-faceted, adaptive innovation culture can help resolve some of the tensions of scaling and growth through various entrepreneurial stages. To help you think more deeply about the types of cultural characteristics that your organization may have and need over time, we turn again to the work of British management philosopher Charles Hampden-Turner, whose theory of dilemma reconciliation was discussed in Chapter 3. In his book *Riding the Wave of Innovation* (2010), Hampden-Turner proposed we use "culture as the integrator for innovative values," and defined four styles of organizational cultures that tend to exist.

Comparing the different characteristics of start-up vs. larger organization

- Typical behaviors of start-ups: Creative, entrepreneurial, risk taking, responsive to change, nimble, cohesive, highly-motivated

---

- Typical behaviors of established organizations: Systematic, efficient, competitive, well managed, profitable, sustainable

---

There are four cultural types/quadrants:

EGALITARIAN

CULTURAL TYPE 1 – Incubator
A culture that is egalitarian, "flat" in terms of hierarchy, and person-centered, suitable at the idea-incubating and nascent startup stage; typical of Silicon Valley.

CULTURAL TYPE 2 – Guided Missile
A culture that is egalitarian and task-oriented, team's effort is focused on getting the tasks accomplished. It is critical to have a culture with deep technical competence to swiftly transform innovative ideas into finished products and move venture creation forward to the next stage.

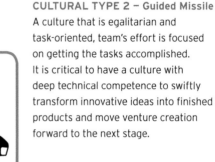

PERSON CENTERED ⟵ ⟶ **TASK CENTERED**

CULTURAL TYPE 3 – Family
A culture that is person oriented and hierarchical, suitable for many family-owned businesses and entrepreneurial small and medium-sized enterprises. The founder often regards his or her employees as members of the family in which mentoring, coaching, trust, and loyalty are essential cultural attributes. Family cultures are hard to maintain when the number of employees grows to more than a hundred.

CULTURAL TYPE 4 – Eiffel Tower
A highly structured culture with clear division of labor. This culture is suitable when the founding members of the innovation team need to manage and lead. Formalizing strategy, structure, system, processes, and control become important to execute repetitive and detailed tasks such as manufacturing of standardized or mass-customized products with precision, high speed, and cost efficiency.

HIERARCHAL

I believe that the four different types of cultures are interdependent and synergistic. Components of each can be creatively combined to resolve organizational tensions during scaling, depending on the DNA and needs of your business. For instance, combining Incubator and Guided Missile cultures creates a Guided-Incubator culture necessary to use market and customer feedback and make fast error and correction iterations to keep customers happy. If you were to apply both the Incubator and Eiffel Tower cultures, you would help create a creative structured, nimble workplace that is responsive to change and remains fiercely competitive. Alternatively, a hybrid of the Guided Missile and Family cultures would produce the professional Guided-Family culture necessary to lower employee turnover and maintain efficiency throughout the scaling stage. Synthesizing the Family culture with the Eiffel Tower would reorganize a family-type enterprise to make it more efficient and cost effective.

If the founders focus on building a sustainable culture to increase organizational capacity to scale the enterprise, the culture can help people better manage transitions and relieve the many tensions that come with scaling.

STAY FOCUSED AND COMMITTED

The founding team's aspirations, persistence, adaptability, and entrepreneurship and your organization's relentless support and commitment are vital drivers for your venture scaling efforts. Renewing the confidence and support of your key strategic partners such as your funding partners, suppliers, and key customers is an important driver at your venture's early stage to begin to form a critical mass of volume for cost efficiency.

 **[_Case in Point_]**   SCALING A MOBILE BANKING VENTURE IN AFRICA

Beth Cobert, Brigit Helms, and Doug Parker wrote an interesting case in *McKinsey on Society* (May 2012) titled "Mobile Money: Getting to Scale in Emerging Markets." The article said that more than a billion people in emerging and developing markets carry cell phones but have no formal bank accounts to conduct their daily financial activities. Mobile banking has taken off rapidly in many parts of Africa with more than 100 mobile-money ventures to fill this gap by offering simple person-to-person or more complex banking transactions over mobile phones, allowing the formerly "unbanked" to enjoy financial services from the palm of their hand.

However, only a handful of these ventures succeed and have reached a sustainable scale, such as M-Pesa in Kenya, MTN in Uganda, Vodacom in Tanzania, and FNB in South Africa. The successful companies do a very good job of managing the agent network, where agents act as the face of the company helping to conduct the cash-in/cash-out functions, and converting cash into electronic money and back again in convenient locations. They developed an adequate agent network before launching the service, providing incentives through commission earnings and agent on-site training. They were able to go to market with a focused killer-application product based on customers' real pain points, whether it be a simple safe and low-cost method to transfer money, or handle international remittances, savings, micro loans, mobile payroll or bill payment. Considerable marketing efforts are required to build a base of frequent users. It is also important not to dilute messaging by diversifying too quickly into other platforms or products too quickly. Finally the report stated that at least three to five years are required to get to scale, so successful companies have to be committed to stay the course with funding until it reaches scale.

ADDRESSING REAL-WORLD TENSIONS THROUGH THE TAO

This chapter thus far covers tips to keep in mind as you scale your business, which is typically the most difficult but integral part of generating a critical mass of consumer adoption for your innovation and a reasonable return on your investment. Beyond the technical aspects of expanding your product or service, many organizational conflicts arise when you reach the crossroads at which you must decide which aspects of your original strategy, structure, processes, and even people need to change to meet the challenges of scaling a business. Pressure is intense and tensions arise between short-term and long-term goals. The necessary types of leadership styles and skills shift from those of a founder/entrepreneur to becoming an "entrepreneurial manager," as your business operation becomes much more complex and the number of people you have to manage increases to stretch your span of control. Whether you are an existing firm or a start-up, you will need to secure additional funding and investment to scale.

As you answer this chapter's innovation question, "How do you scale successfully?," be prepared to face tension between the values of:

Keeping it small and retaining total control	**vs.**	**Scaling now to make more money**

Many founding members struggle with the scaling process, because it requires them to relinquish some of the control and equity they had over their venture. The thought of staying "small and manageable" can be alluring for those who fear diluting or losing the DNA that made their innovation unique and successful. Some entrepreneurs and innovators are content with keeping their business at a size they feel is optimal for balancing control, quality, and profits.

Most big dreamers (and their investors) or anyone with a regional, national, or global vision will want to scale a successful innovation as soon as possible. This allows them to take advantage of economies of scale and increase accessibility, exposure, and profits and in most cases, an innovation cannot truly make a positive impact or shift outdated paradigms until they reach a larger scale. However, scaling prematurely has been the demise of many promising start-ups, as seen during the Internet boom in the 2000s when founders scaled as long as they were able to secure sufficient funding or venture capital with lofty sales projections but a lack of sufficient market validation and no clear understanding of customer adoption. Scaling also presents a challenge to leadership: where a small organization might have grown more organically, scaling requires adding professional managerial competencies and skills as well as a system, structure, and process to standardize operating procedures for efficiency. New talent with scaling and operations experience may be brought in to spearhead the effort, causing clashes with the founding team.

To reconcile the tension between scaling now and scaling later, you need to:

Scale when market conditions are favorable after validating your business model hypotheses and customer acquisition model.

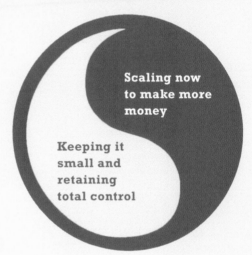

Scaling now to make more money

Keeping it small and retaining total control

Generally speaking, you should not begin scaling your innovation until its business model and value proposition are sufficiently validated and relatively stable. Having learned from your early adopters, who tend to be more tolerant of initial product imperfections, you begin to fine-tune your value proposition and your business model. The focus at this stage is to determine whether you can replicate your business model to attract the early majority segment of the market. Early majority customers make up a much larger group of consumers, who prefer a proven product with little to no bugs, so you will have to ask yourself whether your offering is robust enough to meet the expectations of the early majority. Validating your business model means that the founding team has a good understanding of the metrics involved in getting, keeping, and increasing your customer base and the costs associated with this. You should have also identified, before you scale, the metrics for success in your business model to organize your financial models for scaling. Validating the business model will increase the chances of success whether you scale slowly or quickly. As you grow larger, you will have to manage changes in your culture, which was previously described in this chapter; you will also have to reconcile the expectations of people from multiple cultures, if you want to maintain more control over the direction and growth of the organization. Overall, reconciling these tensions will help your innovation become ready to scale and help you to move one big step closer to fulfilling your innovation dream by building a sustainable company with your novel idea.

HOW ORGANIZATIONS CAN TURN TENSIONS INTO OPPORTUNITIES

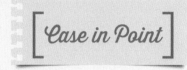

[*Case in Point*] THE PREMATURE SCALING OF WEBVAN

WebVan, an online grocery delivery service, failed very badly during the dot-com bust in 1999 after raising $393 million in funding because it scaled prematurely. It did not carry out adequate testing and iterations of errors and corrections based on market feedback. Instead, WebVan relied on its complex, belt-system, warehousing equipment and facilities, which had high fixed costs. The infrastructure for warehouses were estimated to cost $800 million to $1 billion and had to be built in advance of sales; thus the volumes were uncertain and the business model was unproven. WebVan's business plan estimated 8,000 orders per day. However, when it launched it received only 2,000 orders per day. Moreover, its delivery system was designed to deliver groceries within 30 minutes of an order, but the company failed to realize that many customers preferred deliveries in the evenings when they were home from work. WebVan scaled its business model too quickly in an attempt to "get big fast" and, as a result, went bankrupt in 2001.

On the other hand, Peapod is an example of an online grocery delivery service that scaled successfully. Founded by brothers Andrew and Thomas Parkinson in 1989 in Evanston, Illinois, it is now wholly owned by Dutch world-wide grocery giant, Royal Ahold. For seven years prior to 1996, before the advent of the Internet, Peapod had to provide specific software and dial-up modems to their customers to connect them to the Peapod shopping and delivery system. The two brothers and their families collected the products, packed, and delivered them themselves. Through this family-run business model, they independently expanded to Chicago and its suburbs in 1991, with help from a supermarket chain partner (Jewel-Osco). During the next few years, they also began to partner with a few other chains but only in a few select cities; namely, Safeway in San Francisco, Kroger in Columbus, Ohio, and Randall's in Houston, Texas. During this time the business grew incrementally as its owners learned how to develop the core capabilities that were essential to an online grocery business: testing different business models and software and logistics systems, and working with key partners and communities. When the Internet was born in 1996, Peapod.com was launched. It scaled to new cities across the country relatively slowly, a few at a time, after it tested and iterated its business model and learned about its new customers and markets. The model first spread to Boston, Massachusetts, in 1996, then to Long Island, New York, in 1998, Washington, DC, in 2000 and Virginia and Maryland in 2001 and so on. Since filling its one millionth order in 1998 it has become the leading Internet grocer, delivering more than 23 million orders across 24 US markets. Continuing to evolve its strategy, in 2011, Peapod became the first grocery chain in the United States to launch virtual grocery stores at commuter train stations in several major east coast cities.

How do you scale successfully?

Answering this question starts with the practice of:

Preparing for Rapid Growth

▼ Develop your venture scaling and product adoption plans and strategy.

▼ Compare your scaling plans and strategy to the tips given in the chapter to increase the traction of your product adoption momentum.

Want to go deeper?

Further Reading

Cobert, B., Helms, B. and Parker, D. (2012). "Mobile money: Getting to scale in emerging markets," *McKinsey on Society*, February.

Ries, E. (2011). *The lean startup*. New York, NY: Crown Business.

Blank, S. and Dorf, B. (2012). *The startup owner's manual*. Pescadero, CA: K&S Ranch, Inc.

CHAPTER 9 | YIN-YANG 阴阳

What drives you to innovate?

This element represents "the way" to answer this question.

Yin-yang HARMONIZES between complementary forces. Yin-yang helps you to harness the tensions, conflicting ideas, and dualities you face to achieve a sense of balance and a whole that is greater than the sum of its parts.

Yin-yang represents the practice of Sustaining with Purpose.

OUR FINAL CHAPTER'S KEY INNOVATION QUESTION

What drives you to innovate?

WHY IS THIS QUESTION IMPORTANT?

In the business world, which often focuses on short-term gains and mitigating risk, innovation is a difficult, winding journey that may take years or even decades before you finally reach your desired destination. It is critical to have passion, perseverance, and stamina, but having a deep sense of purpose will be the ultimate guiding force to sustain you throughout your journey. Those driven by only material gain, for lack of a bigger purpose, tend to lose momentum and fizzle out when obstacles throw them off course.

"The true meaning of life is to plant trees, under whose shade you do not expect to sit."

– Nelson Henderson

Despite understanding the key Tao practices of innovation, you will find that sometimes good ideas and solid business plans still don't succeed. Innovation is not an easy journey. Yet leading organizations manage to innovate successfully time and time again. This is not by chance. Innovative thinkers practice certain mindsets that enable them to succeed more often than others. Moreover, after each success, innovators have to work even harder to not fizzle out and sustain growth. Thus, the leaders have to embed these practices into their organizational cultures so that they have long-lasting innovation legacies and stay relevant even in unpredictable futures. Here we present the mindset and practices that are at the heart of sustaining with purpose.

STEPS FOR YOUR ACTION PLAN	WHAT THEY HELP YOU ACCOMPLISH
Be purposeful and passionate	Recognize the central ingredient that drives the innovation cycles
Remember that innovation is not a straight line	Demonstrate how to use the Tao practices in a non-linear fashion
Embody the spirit of innovation	Have an organization that can continuously innovate over the long haul
Use innovation to make a positive impact on the world	Change the world for the better and leave a meaningful legacy

BE PURPOSEFUL AND PASSIONATE

I have met many successful innovators and entrepreneurs across the world. Each innovator is unique, coming from different backgrounds and from across industries, but they have something in common. You may be surprised to know that it isn't wealth. Many successful innovators did not begin as rich and privileged individuals. In fact, many came from ordinary, humble, or even disadvantaged backgrounds. My mantra that I have seen come true repeatedly is that "ordinary people can do extraordinary things." What all successful innovators and entrepreneurs share is a deep passion, not just about their innovation idea, but also how their innovation can have a lasting impact on the world.

Sometimes one's passion and purpose only becomes clear with time or evolves over time. But ultimately, having a deeper purpose requires you to reflect on what change you believe in and are willing to commit to make. It relates to the deeper question of what you want to do with your time on this earth, to better this world, and what legacy you would like to leave behind. This chapter is fitting as the yin-yang center of the Bagua because passion is at the heart of every innovation dream, and drives all the other Tao practices. Strong passion and a sense of purpose is necessary to sustain and adapt to the ups and downs along the treacherous and long path of innovation, including the unpredictability of unplanned events, the disappointments and failures that come with any implementation strategy, the many iterations of errors and corrections, and the lengthy period it takes for you realize your dream.

REMEMBER THAT THE PATH OF INNOVATION IS NEVER A STRAIGHT LINE

While it is true that successful innovators need a deep passion to survive the ups and downs of making change, you also need to realize that the path to innovation is neither direct nor quick. This book has presented the Tao practices in order of the elements within the Bagua to give you a simple and intuitive framework to follow, but in real life, the course is not linear and the various elements do not have to be applied in sequence. I always tell my students, *"Innovation is never a straight line."* Innovation is an ever-dynamic process; this means that as the market forces and environments change, so too must your analyses and strategic plans. You will need to switch between any one of the innovation practices at any time, depending on where you are in the cycle and what challenges you are facing.

As the former dean of a business school, I want to share the story of how the Tao of Innovation practices helped me to reposition and reinvent the Henry W. Bloch School of Management, University of Missouri, Kansas City (UMKC), into a premier School of Management for Entrepreneurship and Innovation during my five-year tenure. Between 2009 and 2014, the Bloch School received national and global top ranking awards for its entrepreneurship and innovation programs in both for-profit and non-profit programs. Today, the Bloch School has emerged as a top-tier School of Management for Entrepreneurship and Innovation nationally.

So how did we get from innovation dream to reality and results? I applied practices of the Tao of Innovation throughout the journey, but they did not play out in a predictable, sequential order. I used them in combination, whenever and wherever they were relevant to the challenges I faced and the tasks I had at hand. A bit of background and historical context first: In 1986, the School of Business and Public Administration at UMKC was endowed by Henry W. Bloch, a Kansas City native, alumni, and the co-founder of H&R Block, the world's largest tax preparation empire. The school was renamed the Henry W. Bloch School of Business and Public Administration, affectionately known to the citizens of Kansas City as "the Bloch School." In 2005, the Kansas City Chamber of Commerce, with the support of city leadership, major businesses, and community leaders, began to seriously discuss and debate the future of Kansas City; specifically how to position it in America and in the world for the 21st century. The conclusion was to make Kansas City a center for health science research, innovation, and entrepreneurship in the Midwest. As a key local institution, UMKC started working closely with the Kauffman Foundation, the world's largest entrepreneurship center also based in Kansas City, to implement a strategy that would help Kansas City realize this aspiration. The first steps were to raise funds to recruit leading scholars in entrepreneurship research and education to begin to build a center of excellence and world-class talent, including the hiring of Dr. Michael Song, the world's leading scholar in Innovation Management Research.

In 2009, the Bloch School began a global search for a new dean to take its school into national preeminence. I was fortunate enough to be hired as the new dean and assumed my role in August of 2009. My first order of business was to **construct a shared View of the Future** and to lay new bets. But before I could do so, I needed to gain firsthand insight into the community I was now a part of and its hopes, fears, and expectations. I devoted my first 100 days of administration to **scanning my environment and inspiring breakthrough ideas**, especially through listening, observing, and sensing the aspirations of our stakeholders, particularly students, parents, alumni, employers, and community leaders. This critical learning time allowed me to understand the external and internal environment that a state school, like UMKC and the Bloch School, competes in and to develop insight into the past, present, and future aspirations of the Bloch School. I needed to determine where the broader future of higher education was heading so that we could carve out our place in it. I put together a steering committee to begin the process of a bottom-up strategic planning, including a broad range of stakeholders from students, faculty, alumni, and administrators. We began to work on **constructing a shared View of the Future**, reflecting the fact that the globalized and Internet world will change the way we educate our young talent. It was clear that traditional methods of learning, where outcomes are focused on content reproduction and analytics, no longer adequately prepared students to compete in a seemingly borderless, globalized world. Furthermore, companies no longer wanted to hire graduates with just high academic scores, but sought out students that demonstrated a "T-shaped" base of knowledge and skills, vertically deep in technical competency, but also horizontally broad in other personal attributes such as the ability to innovate on the job, demonstrate entrepreneurial leadership, function in diverse cross-disciplinary team settings, and compete effectively in a global environment.

Based on our stakeholder insights and View of the Future, we laid the following new bets:

1. Institutions that use the old pedagogical (lecture-based) model alone will be left behind in the 21st century by new on-line educational models and experiential, "learning-by-doing" pedagogy to develop students' ability to apply knowledge quickly and co-create new ideas and solutions in team settings.

2. Employers will hire candidates with deep expertise in technical competencies but also graduates with entrepreneurial leadership, global mindset, and capacity to adapt and innovate on the job, and apply what they learn quickly in a culturally diverse team environment.

Our shared View of the Future and new bets led us to revise our existing mission and vision statements. Our new mission statement changed from providing a "solid preparation in basic management functions with the skills of leadership, entrepreneurship, strategic decision-making" to being repositioned as a "School of Management focusing on Entrepreneurship and Innovative thinking as the foundation for transforming talent and achieving sustainable growth in for-profit and non-profit enterprises." Importantly, the new mission, vision, and value proposition allowed us to **solve our institutional dilemma and tension** about whether we are primarily a School of Business, focused on preparing for managing a business operation, or a School of Public Administration, focused on preparing for the public and non-profit sectors. We reconciled this tension by using the yin-yang approach to dilemma reconciliation: we are both—we have two pillars of excellence in the for-profit management and non-profit management; we aim to nurture the next generation of innovative and entrepreneurial leaders for both the private and public sectors. This also led to the changing of our long-time school name from the Henry W. Bloch School of Business and Public Administration to the Henry W. Bloch School of Management.

Our goal was to become nationally and globally preeminent with a carefully chosen strategic focus and dedicated resources to back it up. In our case, entrepreneurship and innovation was our chosen strategic focus. Our focus is an example of a **smart innovation strategy**, specifically disruptive innovation in the education industry, which faces the same economic, social, and organizational challenges as any other industry. Entrepreneurship and innovation is a relatively new and non-traditional academic field of study, which has not become a formal, mainstream discipline in most American business schools, let alone in other parts of the world. Fewer than 12 business schools out of 1,500 in America today have a stand-alone entrepreneurship and innovation department or offer PhD programs in entrepreneurship and innovation. We boldly chose to compete and make ourselves known in a newly emerging and somewhat disruptive field instead of trying to play catch-up with the old boys in the traditional areas of business education such as finance, marketing, leadership and general management, and operations management, where schools like Wharton, Kellogg, Harvard, and MIT are already well-established winners and commonly recognized centers of excellence respectively.

With the new bets and mission and vision, we set forth to **build a new master plan**, which required a new business design, business model, and business plan. Our business design called for the Bloch School to deepen its innovative strategic position in entrepreneurship and innovation research, education, and service.

We changed our fundamental assumption from that of an urban business school with limited resources and a focus on being accessible to state students to an urban research university's management school that can balance both access and excellence.

Our business design helped to define our new positioning and differentiation strategy across the three dimensions of strategy, operations, and organization. For example, some of the ways we differentiate ourselves from other urban business schools are the types of students we are recruiting (e.g., traditional MBA students, students outside of Kansas City, but also senior executives and corporate teams) which are related to our growth strategy (e.g., recruitment, hiring, infrastructure, etc., to align with the students we want to attract). Our fundamental assumption drove all the strategy formation, and drove the changes to be made across the organization, from a revised student services and alumni involvement and development to new faculty hires. These led to a new business model of how we operate, what we are offering as our key value proposition, and who our target users are. To ensure that we would **ride the wave of opportunity**, we followed the profit pattern of redefining our education product, and who we were targeting to use it (students and executive education).

After crafting our educational business model and strategic positioning, we needed to **pass the stress test.** We began to test the hypotheses in our business model and iterate our strategy before we embarked on scaling the program. First, we examined our internal core resources and capabilities, and we realized we needed to develop more competencies for excellence and to hire more top-notch faculty with entrepreneurship and innovation expertise and in strategic areas of management and non-profit disciplines. We also had to internally reorganize our existing capabilities. In 2010, we established a dedicated department of global entrepreneurship and innovation to house all the entrepreneurship and innovation faculty who previously resided in the marketing department. The Bloch School became one of the

only eight schools in America at that time with a stand-alone dedicated entrepreneurship and innovation department, boasting 12 full-time entrepreneurship and innovation research faculty members. Ultimately, our new bets based on the View of the Future drove our strategy formulation, and all the strategic change initiatives, followed by detailed budgets and implementation timelines. Next, we tested the curriculum in the marketing department and in our institute of entrepreneurship. After initial successful experimentation, we **began scaling** to offer the program widely to students in the engineering, health sciences, law, and music schools. Then we began to increase the adoption rate by offering our "killer application" (i.e. the entrepreneurship and innovation curriculum) widely to all Bloch School undergraduate and graduate students regardless of their major and concentration. Today, our entrepreneurship and innovation courses are the most popular course on campus amongst undergraduate and graduate students outside the Bloch School.

When it came to the time to communicate our vision and strategy, and upon reflecting on our deeper purpose, we chose to use a human-centered story-telling approach by creating a "living mission and vision digital story board" about what the Bloch School would look like in the future if our aspirations were to become a reality in the next 10 to15 years. This digital story board has been revised and can be revised and updated continuously since it was first crafted as a living and unfolding story about our dreams and accomplishments going forward. It centers on the three aspirations of "becoming one of the best entrepreneurship and innovation schools in the world" (in for-profit and non-profit sectors), "propagating learning-by-doing pedagogy for entrepreneurship and management education" and for our students to be "more like Henry W. Bloch each day". Our vision captures the spirit of our benefactor, his hard work, integrity and values, building a business that benefits all people touched by it, persevering through failure and hardship, and giving back generously to the community which nurtured him.

The relentless pursuit of our organizational mission and vision, with all members of faculty, staff, students, alumni, and community behind us began to show results. In 2011, the *Journal of Product Innovation Management* ranked UMKC as the top innovation management research university in the world, based on the faculty's innovation management productivity and research impact. The journal also ranked the Bloch School's two top entrepreneurship and innovation research faculty as the world's number one and number four innovation management research scholars. The Princeton Review ranked both of the Bloch School's entrepreneurship and innovation undergraduate and graduate programs among the nation's top 20. In 2012, US *News and World Report* ranked the Bloch School's non-profit management program as among the nation's top 15 programs. The United States Association for Small Business and Entrepreneurship awarded the Bloch School's entrepreneurship and innovation MBA program

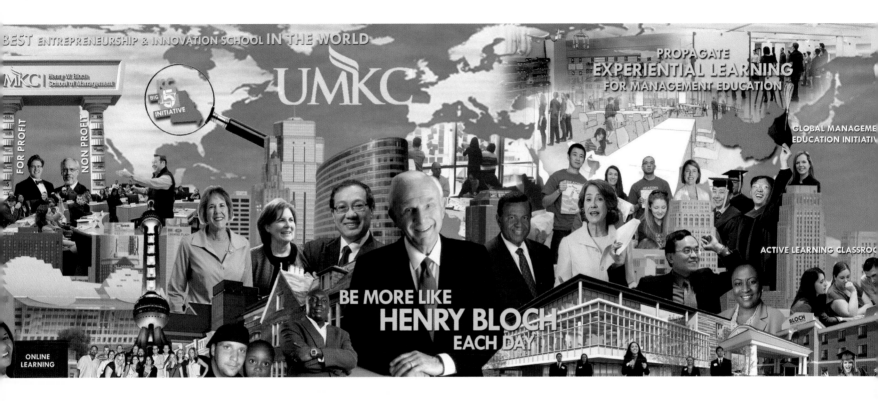

as the National Model MBA Entrepreneurship program in 2010 and its undergraduate program as the National Undergraduate Model Entrepreneurship program in 2014. With all the ranking success and peer recognition, we demonstrated that we had passed the stress test of our novel idea surviving in the real world.

In continuation with **preparing for rapid growth** of our innovation and vision, in August 2013, the Bloch School announced the opening of a new $32 million, state-of-the art, experiential learning or learning-by-doing

teaching facility generously endowed by our benefactor, Mr. Henry W. Bloch. We were privileged to work with two outstanding American Institute of Architects (AIA) award-winning architecture firms and leaders in sustainable design namely, BNIM, Kansas City, MO and Moore, Ruble and Yudell Architects and Planners, Santa Monica, CA. I had the opportunity to work closely with the chief architects and co-founders of both firms, Steve McDowell and Buzz Yudell, their outstanding design teams, and nationally recognized building contractor, JE Dunn of Kansas City, MO to translate a unique vision into an award-winning building to promote entrepreneurship and innovation education.

To **inspire a breakthrough design**, we used analogous inspiration and studied and toured the best and most innovatively designed buildings including management schools, architecture schools, corporations, and design firms such as IDEO in Palo Alto, CA, which are known for having workspaces that successfully nurture creativity and collaboration. It is a 70,000-square-foot building designed to propagate an experiential, learning-by-doing teaching pedagogy. The building is filled with open-concept classrooms with flexible furniture for team settings and has generous whiteboard spaces at the sides, front, and back of the classrooms. The second floor of the new building is a one-of-a-kind, design-led innovation lab equipped with a design studio, market simulation labs, brainstorming room, and prototyping facility to encourage students to iterate their ideas and test their convictions before going to market. It also provides space for accelerators to help incubate high-growth scalable student ventures. This one-of-a-kind building, named the Henry W. Bloch Executive Hall for Entrepreneurship and Innovation, was a very conscious, strategic move to raise the profile of our school, create a learning environment that matched our unique new vision and beliefs, reflect our **deeper collective purpose**, and help us scale our new model of education to set a new standard for management education and to change the world.

I am able to tell this story of success with great pride, but I also faced many barriers and cross-roads every step of the way. My drive to lead, strategize, and implement were constantly tested by diverse views amongst stakeholders, the expectations of the community, limited finances and time—the list goes on and on. But I believe that it was the principles and practices of the Tao of Innovation that allowed me to remain focused on the big picture and end goal. Because I asked the right questions, I was able to build support, make a grand and complex challenge more manageable, ignite passion, and drive our team to collectively discover the answers.

EMBODY THE SPIRIT OF INNOVATION

Successful innovators are not only passionate and able to adapt well to the non-linear innovation journey, they also embed innovation into their way of thinking and their mindsets. They do not define innovation as the core objective, but understand that it is the outcome. They understand that innovation doesn't usually succeed from a top-down directive "to be innovative," but rather from a vibrant culture of innovation evident in its spirit and daily behaviors. Intentionally cultivating this spirit will help you to build an organization with a lasting legacy of innovation as part of its DNA, instead of an innovation "one hit wonder." When innovation is in the fabric of an organization's culture, it will foster people and ideas that strive for continual improvement and evolution. If you or your organization does not nurture this spirit, innovative people and their ideas will always find themselves swimming against the current and eventually take their talents somewhere else. Here are three ideas that lie at the heart of practicing purposeful innovation in a way that makes a difference and is sustainable.

Want to go deeper?

Further Reading

Bloch, T. (2011). *Many happy returns*. Hoboken, NJ: John Wiley & Sons, Inc.

Bloch, T. (2008). *Stand for the best*. San Francisco, CA: Jossey-Bass.

Chang, R. (2000). *The passion plan*. San Francisco, CA: Jossey-Bass. Hampden-Turner, C. (2009). *Teaching innovation and entrepreneurship*. Cambridge: Cambridge University Press.

Kelley, T. and Littman, J. (2005). *The ten faces of innovation*. New York, NY: Currency/Doubleday.

Embrace failing forward

The path of innovation is never a straight line. It is an iterative process of making rapid errors and corrections. Before the Wright brothers took their historic flight in the world's first successful airplane in 1903, they created countless flawed prototypes, suffered many setbacks, and made several failed attempts before finally succeeding. If you are making real change, there will be no precedents, no guarantees, and no perfect outcomes. Perfection paralyses innovation.

Successful innovators "fail forward" in that they accept mistakes as a necessary part of the learning process. They embrace the wisdom gained, are willing to invest in learning experiences, rather than fearing the resources lost on a failed attempt. At the same time, they don't make the same mistake twice and quickly fold their learnings into the next iteration. Rather than waiting for a product to be 100% perfect (it never will be), innovators launch ideas into the market first, knowing that user feedback and market response will guide their evolution. They approach all ventures as ongoing experiments.

2

Be willing to reinvent yourself time after time

Most established companies do not last for more than 30 years because they are motivated to start the process of innovation to rise and compete, but stop once they are ahead. Innovation is an infinite loop, a dynamic process that never ends. In fashion, for example, due to the seasonal and fickle nature of the fashion industry, the designers of top brands can never afford to stop reimagining and redesigning their brands and products. Every season presents the intense pressure but also the opportunity to be provocative and unique, yet on trend, while still remaining true to the legacy and core values of a brand.

Don't become a victim of your own success by thinking, "Why fix something if it's not broken?" We know the only constant is change and over time, customer priorities, business environments, and the structure of an industry never remain static. It is critical to continually ask yourself how the View of the Future is changing, and what new bets need to be laid when you are still on top, not when you've already lost your way. If you practice innovation as a virtuous cycle, you will naturally become your own best competitor.

Nurture a culture of innovation beyond the individual

Too often, innovation comes in the form of a singular great innovative leader or big idea. In these fragile situations, a change of leadership can spell the end of a company's innovative era. General Electric's Jack Welch, Microsoft's Bill Gates, and Apple's Steve Jobs are good examples; many doubt whether the boldness and ingenuity of these companies can be sustained without these visionaries at the helm. In contrast, Google is a great example of what happens when innovation is consciously woven into the fabric of an organization's culture through its mission and vision, hiring practices, management culture, working environment, and daily way of getting work done and collaborating. Google has been well known for giving engineers 20% time (a full day a week) to pursue personal projects they are passionate about. Many of their new products and product improvements have come from the resulting inspiration these employees develop and pursue.

For innovation to be sustainable over long periods of time rather than being sporadic and random, leaders and employees must nurture a culture of innovation. An innovative culture includes empowered employees learning together (not top-down), a collective optimism (not critical and nay-saying), and a collaborative and team-based environment (not competitive and territorial). It must be embedded in an organization's day-to-day process and values. This will ensure that you have built a lasting legacy with innovation as part of your DNA rather than an innovation "one hit wonder."

ADDRESSING REAL-WORLD TENSIONS THROUGH THE TAO

This final chapter is about innovating with purpose and thinking not just about the bottom line but the greater impact your innovation can have on society. As you move forward, I hope you will pursue innovation that improves the way we go about our lives, advances civilization, or makes the world a better place. However, beyond all good intentions, every organiza- tion and business still needs to generate wealth. Without profit, a business cannot continue to operate and contribute to society and the economy.

As you answer this chapter's innovation question, "What is the deeper purpose that drives you to innovate?," be prepared to face tension between the values of:

Maximizing profit	vs.	Creating positive impact (social/environmental)

Most capitalist economies have come to equate success with individu- alistic wealth creation. As a business or organization, your decisions and actions are constantly influenced by pressure to be the market leader, show profits and growth, and meet or exceed targets and shareholder expecta- tions. This can result in making money at any expense and by any means, often to the detriment of workers, the environment, and society. Any resources devoted to "doing good" are then perceived as adversely affect- ing the bottom line.

In the conventional corporate world, making a positive impact is either overlooked, an afterthought, or lost in the politics of corporate social responsibility programs. In the past, making positive contributions to soci- ety and "giving back" was largely handled as an extra step, but more and more organizations are building it into the core of their business models. Beyond providing actual products and services that are designed to help people live better, a positive impact can also take the form of providing employees with good benefits, supporting worthy causes, or reducing the environmental footprint throughout your product's life cycle.

RECONCILING THE TENSION

Creating positive impact (social/environmental)

Maximizing profit

To reconcile the tension between commercial success and doing good, you need to:

Create wealth for individual, corporate, and social good.

More and more businesses are proving that it is possible to benefit themselves, their communities, and society at the same time. Innovations such as micro financing banks, like the Nobel Prize-winning Grameen Bank, help provide loans to the rural poor in impoverished countries to empower them to start businesses and overcome poverty. Sustainable grocery stores, such as Whole Foods, believe in supporting sustainable farming, using eco-friendly materials, and following environmentally sound practices for their energy supply and waste management. Tom's, a shoe company, donates a new pair of shoes to a child in need for every pair of shoes purchased. Conscious consumers and more and more of the younger generations expect more of brands nowadays. It is not enough for a business to exist purely for the sake of making profit.

In his book *Finite and Infinite Games*, theologian and writer James P. Carse states that two types of games exist in the universe: finite and infinite. The objective and conclusion of finite games is winning (think sports, card games, races, competitions). The rules remain constant and enforced. When you win, your competition loses—it is a zero-sum game. Infinite games, in contrast, are played to keep the game going and remain open-ended, with rules and boundaries constantly being redefined. Life itself is an infinite game, so is technology and evolution. Players aim to explore, include other players, and expand the game to move the collective goalpost forward.

The corporate and business world is based on the thinking that innovation is about playing a finite game, where there is a defined pie of wealth, and you play to win and get a bigger piece of the pie.

This results in reshuffling the wealth and resources in society to the winners. My Cambridge University Professor Dr. Charles Hampden-Turner in his book "Mastering the Infinite Game" (1997) states that if innovation can be seen more like an infinite game, business can evolve beyond the prevailing win-lose mentality. Winners and losers both make a positive contribution to advancing the game. Winners redefine the rules and indirectly "teach" losers the rules of the new game, and losers can become future winners. Losers also contribute their learnings—through trial and error—to the advancement of the infinite game. The cycle continues because the game is never-ending. It is a blend of competition and cooperation.

By playing both the finite and infinite game together, innovation can be a force of positive evolution, to improve lives, sustain the planet, advance human civilization, create positive social impacts, and make the world a better place. Social entrepreneurship epitomizes the synthesis of the finite game and infinite game, where you can achieve both wealth creation for the individual and give back for the good of society. More and more organizations need to measure their success against a triple bottom line (a phrase first coined by British sustainability consultant John Elkington), which creates a new standard of delivering goods and services that are simultaneously good for profit, people, and the planet.

Reconciling this tension can be as simple as donating some of the profits from successful businesses to charity and causes that improve the world, as the examples mentioned above indicate. Prolific successful business people such as Bill and Melinda Gates, Michael Bloomberg, and Henry W. Bloch have created a lot of wealth and changed our lives in many ways through their innovations and entrepreneurial spirit. They give back much of their wealth through philanthropic, non-profit causes to communities in need that they have a passion to serve. These communities may be literally in their own "backyard" with very personal ties, or have a global reach, tackling widespread crises.

- Global focus: The Bill and Melinda Gates Foundation, one of the largest private foundations in the world, funds projects in more than 100 countries to tackle extreme poverty and poor health in developing countries, and the failures of America's education system. As of 2013 Bill Gates has donated $28 billion of his own money to the foundation.

- National focus: Bloomberg Philanthropies encompasses all of the charitable giving on behalf of Michael R. Bloomberg. His philanthropic organization focuses on the arts, the environment, public health, education, and government innovation. Bloomberg Philanthropies is the 18th largest foundation in the United States. Bloomberg was among the top 10 American philanthropists from 2004 through 2011.

- Regional focus: The Bloch family has generously supported numerous institutions that improve the lives of people throughout their local Kansas City area, including three special causes: the Henry W. Bloch School of Management, University of Missouri, Kansas City; the Nelson-Atkins Museum of Arts; and St Luke's Hospital of Kansas City. The Bloch family has donated over $100 million in causes to support their hometown.

But you don't have to be a multi-billionaire to make the world a better place. You can also pursue social entrepreneurship as a business. For example, DonorsChoose.org is a social enterprise founded in 2000 by a 25-year-old history teacher from the Bronx named Charles West. The start-up targets schools serving low-income students and helps them raise funds to purchase much-needed school supplies for student projects. West began by spending his own money to help pay for school supplies for his low-income students. Despite his limited technical skills, he created a website where teachers could post requests for classroom project supplies and any donor could choose to support a favorite project. His site uses a crowd-funding method to allow anyone to support a project for as little as $5. As of 2013, DonorsChoose has raised $225 million from more than 1.2 million donors, helping more than 175,000 teachers fund more than 400,000 class projects across the country. They have benefited more than 10 million kids and counting, and innovated an effective way to improve gaps in the complex education system.

We saved the most important practice by far for our conclusion. In my 30 years of working in corporate America, this practice was never once discussed, but it is in my opinion the most important concept of them all! The practice, as described above, is to use innovation to make a positive impact on the world. The point is not that philanthropy did not exist or that environmental sustainability was not considered important. But these concepts of social good were not factored into our business objectives, nor were they embedded in our business model. The sole focus was on cost, competitiveness, and profitability. Looking back I have realized that these alone cannot sustain the free market economy. Instead, I believe we need to practice capitalism with a conscience. Innovation with a purpose is the engine for capitalism with a conscience and it will help sustain the world. I wrote this book to help innovators to transform the world, but specifically for those who want to make the world a better place. The impact you want to make on the world should be directly linked with achieving your innovation dream and sustaining innovation with a purpose.

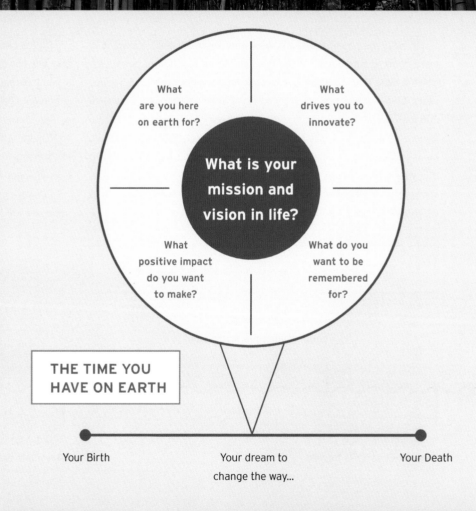

What are you here on earth for?

What drives you to innovate?

What is your mission and vision in life?

What positive impact do you want to make?

What do you want to be remembered for?

THE TIME YOU HAVE ON EARTH

Your Birth

Your dream to change the way...

Your Death

To help you pause and think about the positive impact you want to make, think about yourself in the timeline of the evolution of our planet, which is more than 4.5 billion years old! It wasn't until more than 3.5 billion years later that the first multi-celled organisms were formed. Only until 200 million years ago did the first mammals begin to roam the Earth. *Homo sapiens* as a species didn't roam the earth until 200,000 years ago and human civilization only started to bloom in the Neolithic era, around 8000 BC, when people began to transition from nomadic hunter-gatherer lifestyles to more permanent communities and societies. Human civilization as we know it began thousands and thousands of years ago.

On the one hand, even if you live to be 100 years old, your life will only be a tiny blip in this vast timeline of human civilization. On the other hand, if you look back in time, you will see that advancements in human civilization are composed of individual contributions; of ordinary people doing extraordinary things! You as an innovator also have the chance to make your mark. Think of Einstein, Watson and Crick, Edison, Deng Xiaoping, Michaelangelo... they were all brilliant innovators in their own fields who have changed history.

Innovation is the underlying story of advancing human civilization. I hope you will take the opportunity with your limited time on this earth to

TIME, HISTORY AND YOU IN A FLASH!

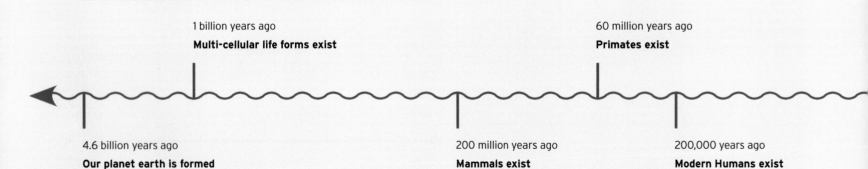

1 billion years ago
Multi-cellular life forms exist

60 million years ago
Primates exist

4.6 billion years ago
Our planet earth is formed

200 million years ago
Mammals exist

200,000 years ago
Modern Humans exist

make the world a better place, in some small or big way. If you are going to embark on the difficult and long journey of innovation, I advise you to combine your drive to innovate with your deeper mission in life. Be purposeful. Having a positive impact on this world requires that you think deeply on your grand purpose in life: for what do you want to be remembered?

Ultimately, innovation is about the pursuit of a dream.

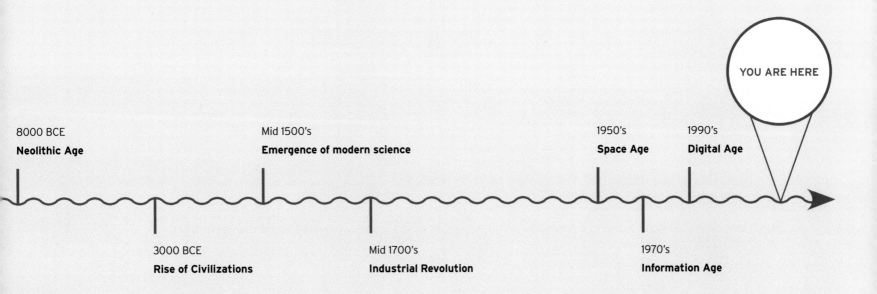

8000 BCE
Neolithic Age

3000 BCE
Rise of Civilizations

Mid 1500's
Emergence of modern science

Mid 1700's
Industrial Revolution

1950's
Space Age

1970's
Information Age

1990's
Digital Age

YOU ARE HERE

This book was a life dream in itself to complete. I hope that my thoughts and concepts help you find the path to live out *your* innovation dream:

I have a dream to change the way…

Throughout the twists and turns of your innovation journeys, use the *Tao of Innovation* to guide your action plan. This is the way to achieve your innovation dream.

9 Key questions every innnovator must answer

1. How is the nature of your business going to change?

2. How do you know when there is an opportunity for innovation?

3. How do you compete to outsmart established players?

4. How do you move beyond the status quo?

5. How do you put yourself in the right place at the right time?

6. How do you craft a strong and lasting go-to-market strategy?

7. How do you know whether your idea can survive in the real world?

8. How do you scale successfully?

9. What drives you to innovate?

9 Key practices to help you find the way to answer them

1. Constructing a view of the future

2. Scanning your environment

3. Crafting a smart innovation strategy

4. Inspiring breakthrough ideas

5. Riding the waves of opportunity

6. Building a master plan

7. Passing the stress test

8. Preparing for rapid growth

9. Sustaining with purpose

About the Authors

TENG-KEE TAN, is the former dean and Harzfeld Professor of Technology Entrepreneurship and Innovation of the Henry W. Bloch School of Management, University of Missouri, Kansas City. He has a BComm from Nanyang University, Singapore, an MBA from the Kellogg School of Management, Northwestern University, and a PhD from the Judge Institute of Management Studies, University of Cambridge. He has been a visiting scholar at Harvard Business School and a visiting professor at China's Nanjing University and Xiamen University. Dr. Tan has combined decades of international corporate experience, entrepreneurial success, and a passion for transformational education to propel the Bloch School of Management to a top-tier institution in the United States in the field of entrepreneurship and innovation. He has directed and taught in senior executive programs around the globe, including the United States, Europe, Singapore, and throughout China. He has consulted for a diverse range of clients across the different types of industries including the consumer products industry. Dr. Tan is the founder of one of the world's first MSc program in Technology Innovation and Entrepreneurship Program. He has also received many teaching awards because he combines the innovation pedagogy of world-renowned academic theory with applied, practical lessons for real-world entrepreneurs and innovators. His life's work is to help illuminate the art and science of innovation to transform individuals and institutions to create a positive, meaningful impact.

HSIEN SEOW, PhD, is a health services researcher and academic at McMaster University, where he teaches palliative care and health system innovation. He is an associate professor in the Department of Oncology, Canada Research Chair in palliative care, cancer, and health system innovation, and Escarpment Cancer Research Institute scientist. He conducts health care research and health care policy reform. He has consulted with health care organizations, regional planners, and ministries of health about health system change across North America. He has taught health system innovation and research methods at McMaster University and the Johns Hopkins School of Public Health. Dr. Seow has a BSc in biology from Yale University and a PhD from the Johns Hopkins School of Public Health. He is currently writing a book focused on health care innovation using the Tao of Innovation principles.

SUE TAN TOYOFUKU is a seasoned design and innovation consultant with executive leadership experience ranging from start-up ventures to Fortune 500 corporations. She began her career as a design strategist and researcher at IDEO, the world's top design and innovation firm and pioneers of the human-centered design thinking methodology. She has consulted for clients across a diverse range of industries, from governments to consumer goods, health care to hospitality and services all over the world. After seven years of consulting in the United States and Asia, she joined the start-up world, serving as Chief Marketing Officer of a mobile app and technology company. She holds a BFA in Industrial Design from the University of Washington, and an MSc in Technology Entrepreneurship and Innovation from Singapore's Nanyang Technological University.

The Tao of Innovation

Nine key questions that every innovator must answer

www.taoofinnovation.org

How is the nature of your business going to change?

How do you scale successfully?

How do you know when there is opportunity for innovation?

How do you know whether your idea can survive in the real world?

How do you compete to outsmart established players?

How do you craft a strong and lasting go-to-market strategy?

How do you move beyond the status quo?

How do you put yourself in the right place at the right time?

FIRE 火

WIND 风

EARTH 地

THUNDER 雷

YIN-YANG

What is the deeper purpose that drives you to innovate?

MARSH 泽

MOUNTAIN 山

阴阳

HEAVEN 天

WATER 水